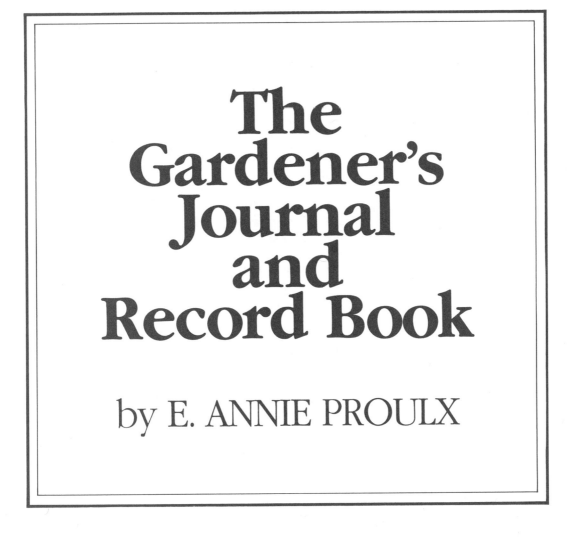

The Gardener's Journal and Record Book

by E. ANNIE PROULX

 Rodale Press, Emmaus, Pennsylvania

Book design by Jeanne Stock
Art direction by Karen A. Schell
Illustrations by Kathi Ember
Photographs of old engravings by Jim Collins

Library of Congress Cataloging in Publication Data

Proulx, Annie.
    The gardener's journal and record book.

    Includes bibliographies.
    1. Gardening—Handbooks, manuals, etc. I. Title.
SB450.96.P76   1983   635   82-24039
ISBN 0-87857-461-1 hardcover
ISBN 0-87857-462-X paperback

2 4 6 8 10 9 7 5 3 1 hardcover
2 4 6 8 10 9 7 5 3 1 paperback

Contents

For my sons—

Jonathan, who transplanted a wild strawberry into the garden;
Gillis, who crawled into a compost heap at a tender age; and
Morgan, who grew enormous radishes.

Introduction

Gardening is an acquired skill. Those experts whose grounds and beds are like a horticultural dream reached that point by combining keen observation, occasional experimentation, and regular record-keeping. Observation and records help you to practice good crop rotation, to identify your microclimate, to know when it is safe to plant outside in your immediate locality through natural phenological indicators. Records show you the steady improvement of garden soil and the increase of harvests; records let you conduct your own field trials of experimental plants. Your records can be worth their weight in rubies to someone who tills the land after you, to plant observers and breeders who need information on the growth and behavior of plants in your area, or even to a yet-unborn agricultural historian seeking to chart shifts in climate, crops, diet, and cultivation techniques.

This book was prepared by a gardener frustrated by messy notebooks, disappointed by the so-called garden record books offered by many publishers that spare room enough to enter only three words under the formidable heading TOMATOES, and bored with the repetition of the same old gardening basics found on the back of every seed packet. This record book gives you concise and richly varied information on how and where to find out what you need to know and gives you plenty of room to write down what is happening in your garden. It encourages experimentation and observation and hopes to pique your curiosity about things horticultural, from saving your own seed to collecting rare books on gardening. This book should be as useful to you as a well-sharpened hoe. It is a garden tool—and is meant to be used as one.

A Word about the Illustrations

The nineteenth century was a period of extraordinarily keen interest in gardening. A flood of books on every aspect of horticulture from exotic plants to rutabaga culture poured from the many agricultural presses. Most of these books were lavishly illustrated with techniques, vistas, designs, plans, tools, and plants. An hour or two with some of these earlier books will show the gardener of today that hundreds of devices and methods designed for sophisticated gardening have passed from the scene. Practices we hail as innovations—such as composting or passive solar greenhouses—were common 150 years ago. Landscaping and the design of homes to fit the site and give the owners privacy and wonderful gardens were very much more highly developed than our efforts with grape stake fences and redwood tubs.

There is much in these old books to interest and excite the modern gardener. The illustrations for this journal have been chosen from some of these old books, not because they are amusing or quaint, but because they instruct and inform us with a richness of detail sadly absent in our own gardening works.

Soil Tests and Problems

Soil is more important to a good garden than anything else except climate, and the gardener who learns the characteristics of his or her soil, then takes the trouble to improve problem soil areas by increasing or releasing nutrients available to the plants, by bettering drainage, by repairing eroded or worn-out soils, by recognizing and correcting common soil problems as a matter of course, is on the way to becoming a master gardener.

You can learn the soils on your property by observation and testing of the soil itself and by noticing the wild plants that grow lustily on certain types of soil habitat. Wild plant field guides will give a soil watcher much help in charting soil characteristics.

Walk your land often, and gradually draw your own soil map based on what you observe—a very useful kind of information when it comes to long-range agricultural or horticultural land-planning use and land improvement. You can blend your detailed observational data with the more general soil survey maps for your county available from the Soil Conservation Service (SCS) of the United States Department of Agriculture (USDA).

Use the blank space on the next page for a soil map of your property.

Soil Types

Three basic soil types—clay, sandy, and loam—give the gardener a rough guide for judging his or her soil. In actuality, the soils on your property will probably be much more complicated, even in a small area. A well-drained grassy slope will have fertile, loamy soil; bottomland along a stream will be quaggy and silty; there will be rich soil high in organic material where the old henhouse once stood; and there may be gullied, eroded, exposed subsoil where chemically fertilized corn was planted for many years. You may face more difficult problems than just conditioning a heavy soil or giving body to a sandy soil. If you have just moved into a new development, the topsoil may have been stripped away by bulldozers in the name of

Soil Conservation Service

One of the most helpful Government agencies is the SCS of the USDA. Their agents can supply you with very detailed soil survey maps for your county and aerial photographs and will help you plan the use and management of your soil at no charge. They will advise you on land drainage techniques, woodland management, road building, pond building, sewage treatment, pasture improvement techniques, and erosion prevention. For the nearest agency, check your telephone directory under United States Government, Agriculture Department, Soil Conservation Service. Your taxes support the SCS—let them help you.

level ground, or topsoil of unknown character trucked in from somewhere else. You may have the daunting job of working up a shale soil or breaking up extremely rocky soil.

These difficult conditions take observation, careful planning, and good record-keeping to plot and illustrate your improvements.

Clay. Clay soils are made up of microscopically tiny particles that pack tightly together. A handful of clay soil will squeeze into a ball and has a greasy feel. Drainage is usually poor, aeration poor, and acid buildup pronounced. By admixing lime or gypsum, organic material, and coarser soils, the structure of a clay is improved and fluffed up, and nutrients are released to make an excellent garden soil.

Sandy. Light and coarse textured, this soil drains so rapidly that nutrients leach out and the poor water supply is a serious problem for growers. Sandy soils are improved by working in organic materials and clay soils.

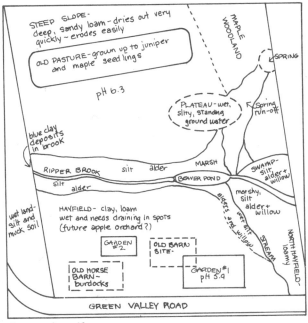

A sample soil map.

Soil Map

Loam. There are all kinds of loams, but generally they are friable, easily worked topsoils that have both good drainage and good capacity for storing plant nutrients. This is the gardener's ideal soil, and though it does occur in nature, it also can be built through soil conditioning.

Potting Soils

You can make your own balanced soil mix for seed-starting next spring. Make it in the late summer or fall, and store it in the toolshed in a plastic garbage can with a cover. This is far superior to the packaged stuff, and the seedlings will have fewer problems adjusting to garden soil than if they were started in a soilless mix. Both the soil and sand should be pasteurized. The job can be done in an oven (a very pungent procedure) or on an outside fireplace.

The best soil base is from an old pasture or hayfield where the soil particles are coated with humus from decaying grass roots—fertile, nearly neutral pH soils that are far better than a late summer flower bed or garden soil.

Here is a recipe for a basic potting mixture: Mix 1 part pasteurized soil, 1 part compost, and 1 part sharp builder's sand. (Do not use stream bank or beach sand—they have been rounded by water action and pack too tightly together. Beach sand has the further disadvantage of saltiness.) Add 1 tablespoon of bone meal for each quart of the mixture. Mix these ingredients thoroughly.

There are potting-soil-mixture recipes to suit the needs of all sorts of house plants and indoor growing situations. For more recipes see *Rodale's Encyclopedia of Indoor Gardening,* edited by Anne M. Halpin (Emmaus, Pa.: Rodale Press, 1980).

To Pasteurize Soil. Put the soil or sand loosely into an enamel or stainless steel baking pan. Add a cup or so of water to make the soil damp but not wet—the steam generated is a major agent of pasteurization. Cover the pan snugly with aluminum foil (some gardeners prefer to use the commercial turkey-size roasting bags for this purpose). Insert a meat thermometer. Hold the soil in the oven at a temperature of 160°F to 180°F for 30 minutes. *Do not overheat.* Cool and use in the potting soil mix.

Use the following page to write down your favorite potting mixture recipes.

Testing Soil

A soil test is not needed every year. If you have an established garden that is doing well and has been for some time, you needn't test it more often than every five years or so. But if the garden soil is an unknown quantity, or if you are having problems with it, a test can help you correct and condition it.

Most state university laboratories give you basic information on soil pH, available phosphorus, reserve phosphorus, available potash, and available magnesium, if specially requested. They will recommend the fertilizers (amounts and types) and the amounts of organic material and ground limestone (if needed) to bring up the pH of an acid soil. If you are growing special crops or plants such as grapes that demand certain soil conditions, mention it on the test application form, and the suggestions for soil modification will be tailored to those needs.

The problem with these tests, available in nearly every state, is that they are run through a computer now, and applicants may check only one box on the questionnaire page of the application form; such limits necessarily make the test results more general than specific. Interpretation of the tests is usually done through your County Extension Agent. If you've got a good agent, keen on gardening and interested in organic soil improvement, he or she can be tremendously helpful in explaining how to make the test results work for you and become part of a long-term soil improvement program.

By comparison, private soil-testing laboratories usually do much more complicated testing and work out fertilization and soil-conditioning programs specifically for a grower's needs. For example, Woods End Laboratory, in Maine, does humus chromatograms that allow an estimate of nitrogen release, as well as cation balance and exchange capacity. They also do compost audits of some complexity and welcome detailed descriptions of the soil and compost problems from the gardener. Costs for such complex tests may be three or four times greater than the basic state soil tests.

How to Take a Soil Sample. It is a good idea to take soil samples at midsummer; the soil is stable and the biological activity at a high point. Spring testing doesn't give you time enough to get the soil conditioned for that season's garden. Fall testing finds the soil fairly exhausted.

To get a really representative soil sample, take soil from up to 20 different points in the plot you are testing. Use a sharp trowel, and *make sure all your tools are clean.*

First, make a hole 6 inches deep.

Second, from the side of the hole take a slice of soil about an inch thick with the trowel.

Soil Tests

Garden/Bed _____   Soil Type & Texture _____

Date Sampled _____   _____

Laboratory _____   _____

Tests	Results	Recommendations	Procedures & Results
Nitrogen			
Phosphorus			
Potassium			
pH			
Other			

Tests	Results	Recommendations	Procedures & Results
Nitrogen			
Phosphorus			
Potassium			
pH			
Other			

Third, measure the slice into thirds with your eye, and, with another trowel or knife, discard the two outer sections, keeping only the central core of the slice.

Finally, mix all the core samples *thoroughly* in a clean bucket. Remove about a cupful of this mixture for the sample, and package it according to the directions from the soil-testing agency you have chosen.

Keep these important points in mind when taking soil samples:

All tools—shovel, bucket, and trowels—and the shipping container should be very, very clean. Residues and foreign material can skew the results of the test.

Do not smoke while taking soil samples. A few flakes of ash can seriously distort the test readings.

Do not take samples from places where manure, compost, lime, or fertilizer were piled.

The soil of the sampled plot should be fairly uniform; try not to mix cores from areas that have very different soils—such as a trowelful from the sandy hillside, another from the boggy bottomland, and another from the place you grew soybeans last year. You can't mix them all together and expect to get a conditioning prescription that will apply to such radically diverse soils.

If you have already spread limestone or phosphate on your soil before test samples are taken, you must wait several months before sampling the soil. Fertilizer applications demand a wait of three or four weeks before sampling.

Don't sample right after a rain—wait a few days. Increased biological action in the soil after a rain can give a false idea of the nutrient level.

Where to Get Soil Tested. Soil-testing laboratories at the state universities test soil at fees ranging from $3.00 to $8.00. Directions and sample mailing bags are available at the County Extension Offices. A list of the addresses for each state university can be found in the Brooklyn Botanic Garden's *Handbook on Soils*, available for $2.85 including postage and handling from: Brooklyn Botanic Garden, 1000 Washington Ave., Brooklyn, NY 11225.

Private soil-testing laboratories are on the increase. Check your Yellow Pages for local labs. Some outstanding soil labs are listed below. Write for sampling instructions and bags.

Woods End Laboratory, RFD Box 65, Temple, ME 04984.

S. R. Sorensen, Prescription Soil Analysis, Box 80631, Lincoln, NB 68501.

Eaton Valley Agricultural Services, C.P. 25, Sawyerville, PQ J0B 3A0, Canada.

Use the preceding pages to record the results of soil tests and the soil improvement measures you undertake to bring the nutrients into balance.

Recognizing Soil Problems

Puddled Clay Soil. Clay soil adsorbs sodium on each microscopic particle, and the sodium tends to attract water. As the water drains through the soil, the particles pack together tighter and tighter until the soil structure eventually becomes airless and dense, and rainwater lies on top of the impermeable surface in puddles. The solution to the problem is to break the chemical bond which makes the sodium cling to the particles. Adding calcium forces the particles to exchange the sodium ions for calcium ions, and slowly the densely packed clay layers separate into crumbs with good air spaces in the aggregate. Slower procedures are *(a)* to add limestone (calcium carbonate), though this will raise the pH of the soil; or *(b)* to work in organic material liberally—compost, green manure, old hay mulch, poplar leaves. The most rapid answer is to add agricultural gypsum (calcium sulfate), which acts quickly and does not affect the pH level.

Acid Soil. Although some western soils are alkaline, a far more common soil problem is acid soil, a condition which chemically locks away nutrients from plants. Vegetables like a pH of around 6.2 to 6.8—just slightly acid. But the pH scale is not as simple as it seems, for the pH numbers from 1 to 14 are not simple arithmetical gradations, but abbreviations for logarithm powers. The exponential numbers of the scale each represent 10 times the value of the preceding number, so that a soil that measures a pH of 5.8 is *10 times* more acid than a soil measuring pH 5.9. A pH of 5.2 is *100 times* more acidic than a pH of 6.2; this is why litmus paper strips are almost useless for testing the acid in soil. Very precise results are necessary to avoid error.

Alkaline Soil. These soils run on the upper side of the pH scale, above neutral 7.0. Ericaceous plants like the rhododendron simply can't stand alkaline soil. If you have soil on the alkaline side, or that is only slightly acid, you can bring down the pH by working in acid soil conditioners such as pine needle mulch, oak leaves, and acid peat.

Soil Problems

Garden/Bed	Soil Problem	Corrections	Results

Garden/Bed	Soil Problem	Corrections	Results

Sometimes, agricultural sulfur or ferrous sulfate is added.

Soluble Salts. Light and frequent waterings, especially to house plants, draw soluble salts to the soil surface, and when moisture in the soil evaporates, the soluble salts are left as a white deposit. Overfertilization and bad drainage contribute to the problem. Seeds germinate poorly in such overloaded soil, and plants are generally sickly. Flushing the soil with plenty of clean water will help the salts leach down out of the immediate root zone.

Iron Deficiency. This malady can smite all sorts of plants, from vegetables to ornamentals. The symptoms are interveinal chlorosis and usually slow, stunted growth. Sandy soils with meager amounts of organic material are prone to this deficiency, as are soilless mixtures. If you dump too much lime or too much phosphorus on your soil, you can chemically lock iron away from your plants. The solution to the problem is to work in more organic material.

Compacted Soil. Compaction is one of the most common garden problems of all. Rototilled soils pack down very easily when walked on, and garden paths trodden into the soil mean poor aeration, reduced yields, and water runoff. On the other hand, permanent wide rows and French Intensive wide beds do not suffer traffic, so the soil always stays loose and friable. If you *must* have trodden garden paths, mulch them heavily—row plants will gratefully extend their roots down into the damp, rich soil under the path. The mulching cushions your footfall and prevents the compaction.

Incompatibility. When seedlings raised in soilless mixtures are set into a garden, they dry out faster than the surrounding soil. As you transplant, gently get rid of some of the soilless mix, then mulch around the plant to retain moisture, and water these plants more frequently.

You can use the preceding pages to note specific soil problems you encounter, how you treat them, and how well your treatments work.

Soil Bibliography

If you find yourself increasingly fascinated by the invisible chemistry of soil and want to know more about this most vital part of gardening, here are some books to get you started:

B. J. Knapp, *Soil Processes.* London: George Allen & Unwin, 1979. This English booklet is extremely well illustrated in color and is a technical review of the physical, chemical, and biological processes that give a soil its character. Difficult reading in places, but contains up-to-date findings on soil processes and is well worth reading.

Gene Logsdon and the Editors of *Organic Gardening, The Gardener's Guide to Better Soil.* Emmaus, Pa.: Rodale Press, 1975. This is a helpful basic text for beginning gardeners.

H. Stuart Ortloff and Henry B. Raymore, *A Book about Soils for the Home Gardener.* New York: M. Barrows and Co., 1962. Although out of print, this book is still one of the best introductions to garden soils and what happens in them. Try your library or inquire from a horticultural book dealer for a copy (see page 190).

Soil, The Yearbook of Agriculture. Washington, D.C.: U.S. Government Printing Office, 1957. An oldie but a goodie, this book is available in most libraries. Though aimed at Midwest agribusiness farmers, there's plenty of useful material here for the home gardener who is serious about soil.

Bette Wahlfeldt, *Successful Sandy Soil Gardening.* Order from the author, General Delivery, Gonzalez, FL 32560. The price is $5.75. This book was written for Gulf Coast gardeners, but is useful to anyone struggling with a sandy soil.

Garden Plans and Designs

Use this section to plot and plan your annual vegetable gardens; to help you decide where shrub and tree placement should be in grounds landscaping; to lay out orchard plantings for maximum pollination; to design an herb garden; to build up perennial borders; to naturalize your property with bulbs—in short, to mark and list every plant you want to keep an eye on. Refer to previous years' vegetable garden plans when you decide where to put the current year's plants for informed crop rotation.

Vegetable Gardens

Nearly every book on basic vegetable gardening includes suggested plans with estimated yields. Several seed supply houses now work out computerized vegetable garden planning charts for customers who fill out questionnaires. Two of the best books offering gardening plan information are:

John Jeavons, *How to Grow More Vegetables Than You Ever Thought Possible on Less Land Than You Can Imagine.* Berkeley, Calif.: Ten Speed Press, 1979. The planting charts, sample record-keeping section, crop rotation suggestions, and the four-year graduated size garden plans make this an almost indispensable aid for beginning gardeners. Experienced gardeners will pick up plenty of ideas.

James Edward Knott, *Handbook for Vegetable Grow-*

ers. New York: John Wiley & Sons, 1957. This older book is still extremely useful.

The Superior Vegetable Garden Site. To pick the best site for your vegetable garden, consider the following:

A southern exposure where at least half the available summer sunlight falls directly on the garden is an ideal location.

If your land is hilly, place the garden high on a gentle slope so cold air drainage will not affect the soil and ground temperatures unduly.

Wind protection in the form of windbreaks that are 50 percent permeable, such as snow fencing, picket fence, or willow or deciduous hedges, will protect plants from wind chill and lessen the chances of soil loss through wind erosion.

Good soil drainage is important. Soil conditioning will improve drainage, and a slight slope will help excess water run away. Unimproved clay soils or putting the garden in a low-lying area will mean poor drainage and cold, wet, infertile soil.

Good soil; a friable, loamy soil rich in organic material and with an optimum pH is the basic foundation of a good garden.

Put the garden near your house, for it will get better care and benefit from constant observation and the quick recognition of problems.

Choose the best microclimate on your property. Observation and record-keeping will tell you where the sunniest, most sheltered place on your property lies; where the frost leaves early and arrives late; where the soil responds readily to your ministrations.

For pages to keep detailed records of your vegetable crops, see From Seed to Harvest, page 84. Use the pages that follow to plan your vegetable gardens. You can sketch out planting arrangements that make the best use of site and space and also plan successions and rotations. The grids on these planning pages and others that you'll find throughout this section will enable you to draw your garden layouts to scale if you wish. Let each block of the grid stand for a unit of space in the actual garden. A block could equal 6 inches, for example, or 1 foot.

The prickly cardoon was a salad vegetable much favored in France in the nineteenth century. It demanded a long growing season and was blanched by tying up the leaves loosely and then wrapping them in straw. Because of the spiny leaves, special cardoon sticks joined by twine were used to pull the leaves together, as shown here.

Fruit Trees

Whether you plant a pair of flowering crab trees outside your door or an orchard of apples, plums, and pears, careful planning on paper is a necessity before you order. Growing fruit at home is tremendously rewarding and can supply you with sweet cider, juices, and loads of fruit for canning, drying, and eating fresh. Grafting and propagation of fruit trees can become an absorbing hobby. You might like to specialize in new disease-resistant varieties, to collect the old heirloom fruits, or to try dwarf trees or experimental hardy cultivars.

One of the most advanced sources of high-quality fruit trees and small fruits is the New York State Fruit Testing Cooperative Association, Inc., Box 462, Geneva, NY 14456. Old varieties, standard cultivars, and new and experimental fruits are offered by NYSFTA, and members of the association may participate in trials of unnamed cultivars. An annual Member's Day features expert speakers on fruit problems and tours of the Geneva

PLUMBS—50 Cents.

† Denotes large size.
* ———— superior flavour.

Jaune hative, or early yellow	*ripe in July.*
Chicasaw	do.
*Early scarlet, or cherry	August.
Early damask, or Morocco	do.
Precoce de Tours	do.
Golden drop } These are beautiful native {	do.
Early coral } fruits suitable for preserves {	
Azure hative	do.
*Early sweet damson	do.
Fotheringham	September.
Blue perdrigron	do.
German prune, *Guetsche* \$1	do.
Red imperial	do.

Here are listed a few of the 44 plum cultivars offered by the Mills Nursery on Long Island in 1825. Their selection of 42 varieties of cherries, 78 of pears, 64 peaches, 33 kinds of gooseberries, 205 rose cultivars, and much more show the rich range of choices our ancestors enjoyed. Our comparatively meager fruit catalogs, even those from specialty nurseries (though lavishly illustrated), list far fewer choices in fruit varieties.

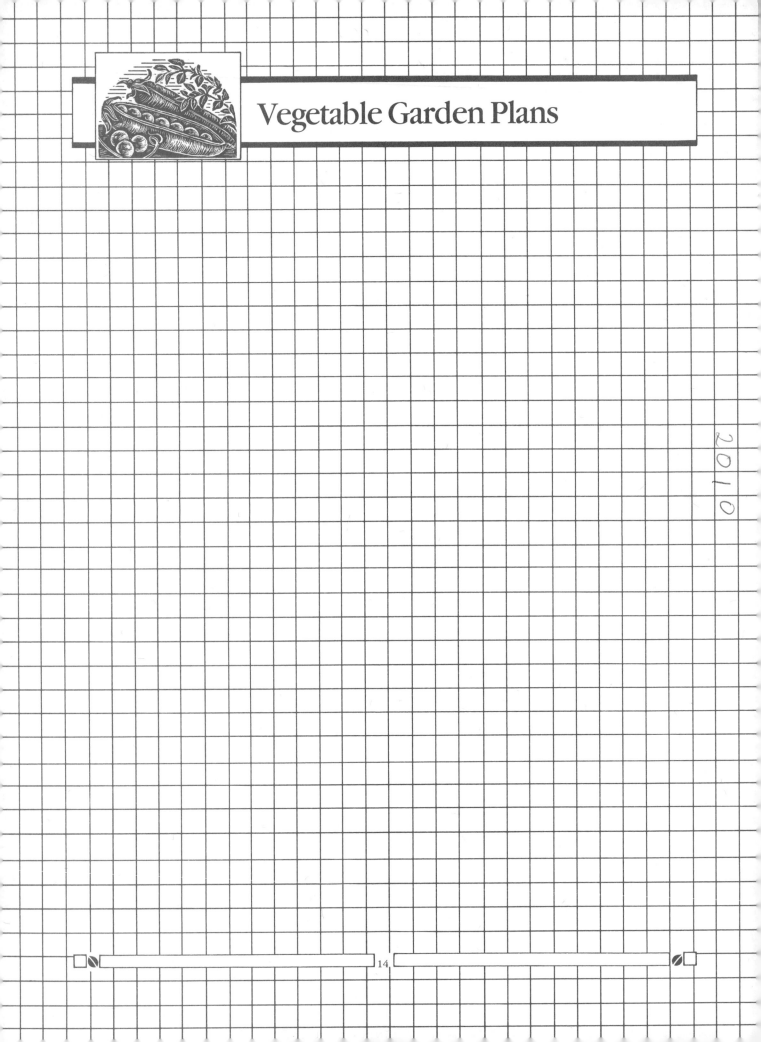

Vegetable Garden Plans

2010

orchards, including the famous orchard where more than 1,000 different cultivars of apple are maintained in a living museum.

Fruit Varieties Journal is published by the American Pomological Society, 103 Tyson Bldg., Pennsylvania State University, University Park, PA 16802. Membership in the society is $10 per year. For news of old and uncommon types of fruit that home growers around the country are cultivating, you'll want to read *Pomona,* published quarterly by the North America Fruit Explorers (NAFEX), 10 S. 055 Madison St., Hinsdale, IL 60521. Membership is $5 in the U.S.; $7 in Canada and elsewhere.

The following Agricultural Extension Services offer unusually rich information on fruit growing, for they are allied with institutions where fruit growing is important:

University of California, Davis, CA 95616.

University of Illinois, Urbana, IL 61801.

University of Massachusetts, Amherst, MA 01002.

Michigan State University, East Lansing, MI 48823.

Rutgers University, New Brunswick, NJ 08903.

New York State College of Agriculture, Ithaca, NY 14853.

Ohio State University, Columbus, OH 43210.

College of Agriculture, Pennsylvania State University, University Park, PA 16802.

For information on Canadian experimental fruit testing stations and nursery sources, write:

Horticultural Research Institute, Vineland Station, Ontario, Canada.

There are many excellent books on fruit tree and small fruit growing. One of the most helpful is:

Brooklyn Botanic Garden Handbook No. 67, *Fruit Trees and Shrubs.* Order from Brooklyn Botanic Garden, 1000 Washington Ave., Brooklyn, NY 11225.

Use the following pages to keep cultural records on your fruit trees. Since trees are more or less permanent additions to the landscape, diagram their locations on your overall landscape plans, pages 28 to 31. But use the grid on page 21 to figure out the spacing, which is very important to ensure good pollination.

In the mid-nineteenth century, M. Lèpere of the Paris suburbs was called "the emperor of peach-growers." His famous Napoleon peach tree spelled out the conquering hero's name against a whitewashed wall in his gardens. No less dramatic is this series of eight trained peach trees which spelled out the grower's name against a very high white wall. This virtuoso (if somewhat vulgar) display attracted visitors from all over the world.

Fruit Tree Record

Species & Cultivar	Rootstock	Source	Date Planted	Date Propagated	Cultural Notes
Akane Apple					
Liberty Apple					

Species & Cultivar	Rootstock	Source	Date Planted	Date Propagated	Cultural Notes

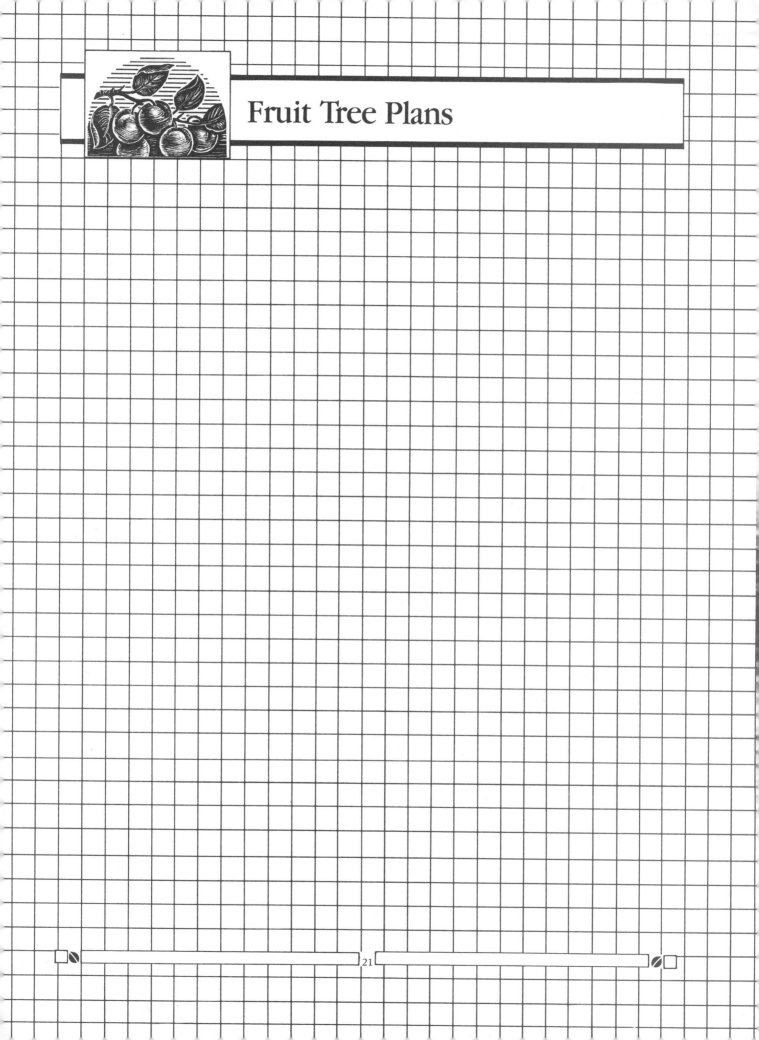

Fruit Tree Plans

Small Fruits and Berries

Lewis Hill's *Fruits and Berries for the Home Garden* (New York: Alfred A. Knopf, 1977) remains the best beginner's guide to growing home fruits, from apples to gooseberries. Also helpful is *All About Growing Fruits and Berries* (San Francisco: Ortho Books, 1977). For detailed information on cultivars and cultural procedures best suited to your region, see the bulletins of the nearest Agricultural Extension Service.

Many nurseries deal in fruit and berry stock. Here are some of the best known:

Stribling Nursery, 1620 W. 16th St., Box 793, Merced, CA 95340.

The Hudson River Antwerp raspberry, a popular market variety in 1867.

Armstrong Nurseries, Box 473, Ontario, CA 91761.

L. E. Cooke Co., 26333 Rd. 140, Visalia, CA 93277.

Bunting's Berries, Selbyville, DE 19975.

Lawson's Nursery, Rt. 1, Ball Ground, GA 30107.

Ison's Nursery & Vineyard, Brooks, GA 30205.

Owen's Vineyard and Nursery, Georgia Hwy. 85, Gay, GA 30218.

Whatley Nursery, Rt. 1, Box 197, Helena, GA 31037.

Bountiful Ridge Nurseries Inc., Princess Anne, MD 21853.

W. F. Allen Co., Box 1577, Salisbury, MD 21801.

Rayner's Bros., Inc., Salisbury, MD 21801.

Southmeadow Fruit Gardens, 2363 Tilbury Place, Birmingham, MI 48009.

Dean Foster Nurseries, Hartford, MI 49257.

Hilltop Orchards & Nursery, Rt. 2, Hartford, MI 49057.

Grootendorst Nurseries, Lakeside, MI 49116.

Miller's Nursery, Canandaigua, NY 14424.

Kelly Brothers Nurseries, Dansville, NY 14437.

New York State Fruit Testing Cooperative Association, Inc., Box 462, Geneva, NY 14456.

Mayo Nurseries, Route 14, Lyons, NY 14489.

Bowers Berry Nursery, 94959 Hwy. 99 E, Junction City, OR 97448.

Weeks Berry Nursery, 6494 Windsor Island Rd. N, Salem, OR 97303.

Adams County Nursery & Fruit Farm, Aspers, PA 17304.

Heath's Nursery, Box 707, Brewster, WA 98812.

Buckley Nursery Co., Rt. 2, Box 199, Buckley, WA 98321.

C. D. Schwartze Nursery, 2302 Tacoma Rd., Puyallup, WA 98731.

C & O Nursery, Box 116, 1700 N. Wenatchee Ave., Wenatchee, WA 98801.

The following pages can be used for keeping cultural records on your small fruits and berries. You can diagram your berry patch right on the master landscape plans, on pages 28 to 31, and use the grid on page 25 to calculate the spacings of the individual plants or bushes.

Small Fruits and Berries Record

Species & Cultivar	Source	Date Planted	Cultural & Propagation Notes
Blueberries			Fertilized with 10-20-20 April 2, 1986

Species & Cultivar	Source	Date Planted	Cultural & Propagation Notes

Small Fruits and Berries Plans

Landscaping

After decades of landscaping books that feature vast, unproductive green lawns to set off clusters of bulbs and exotic flowering shrubs, fresh new winds are blowing. Unmowed wildflower lawns, landscaping to improve wildlife habitat, landscaping to harmonize with the natural environment, and decorative plantings of useful, food-producing plants are beginning to appear and make their mark on our surroundings. Listed in this section are not only the standard older landscaping sources, but some of the new trailblazing books that mark the shift toward naturalistic landscaping.

Correspondence Courses. Half a dozen universities offer correspondence courses in horticulture and agriculture, and many include landscaping courses in their mailbox curriculum. See a fuller listing on page 69. The University of Guelph in Ontario, Canada, has long had an outstanding reputation for landscape design and offers a number of first-rate correspondence courses on the subject. Available courses include Plant Use in the Home Landscape, Landscape Graphic Techniques, Landscape Design and Installation, Indoor Landscaping, and Fundamentals of Garden Design.

For more information and enrollment applications write:

Independent Study, Office of Continuing Education, University of Guelph, Guelph, ON N1G 2W1, Canada.

Professional Help. If you want advice on choosing the services of a professional landscape architect, write to:

The American Society of Landscape Architects, 1750 Old Meadow Rd., McLean, VA 22101. This organization publishes a quarterly magazine, *Landscape Architecture.*

Help from the Government. An outstanding book on landscaping is Gary B. Robinette's *Plants, People and Environmental Quality,* put out by the American Society of Landscape Architects Foundation and the U.S. Department of the Interior. It costs $4 and can be ordered from:

Superintendent of Documents, U.S. Government Printing Office, Washington, DC 20402.

Other pamphlets, booklets, and charts on home landscaping can be found in List 5, *Popular Publications for the Farmer, Suburbanite, Homeowner and Consumer* and List 11, *Available Publications of the USDA.* Order both from the Superintendent of Documents.

Classes, leaflets, bulletins, packets, and posters on

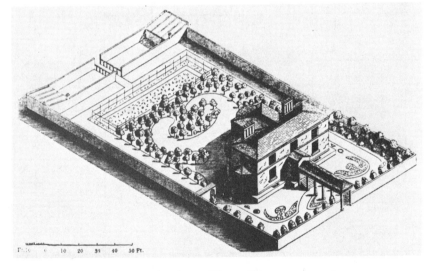

This 1850 plan for a suburban villa on 1¾ acres contains a remarkable assortment of gardens. At the back of the house is an attached semicircular greenhouse. An arabesque lawn is ornamented with trees and flower beds. Behind the house is a fruit garden— strawberries, gooseberries, currants, and raspberries—surrounded by a border of cherries, plums, and pears. At the back are two heated pits for forcing early vegetables and greenhouse plants, with room below ground for growing mushrooms!

gardening, landscaping, and horticulture keyed to your region are available from the Cooperative Extension Service in your state. Home gardeners have become the major focus of Extension Service personnel in recent years.

Books to Aid in Landscaping. An hour or two browsing in a good library or bookstore can introduce you to the extraordinarily varied approaches to home landscaping. Here are a few basic books that can guide you from a bare plot to rich and flowery bowers.

David Hicks, *Garden Design.* London: Routledge & Kegan Paul, 1982.

Donald Wyman, *Trees for American Gardens,* rev. ed. New York: Macmillan, 1965.

_____, *Shrubs and Vines for American Gardens,* rev. ed. New York: Macmillan, 1969.

The following Brooklyn Botanic Garden handbooks offer concise landscaping information for a modest price—$2.85 each: No. 36, *Trained and Sculptured Plants;* No. 49, *Creative Ideas in Garden Design;* No. 65, *Tree and Shrub Forms—Their Landscape Use;* and No. 84, *Small Gardens for Small Spaces.* Order the BBG handbooks from:

Brooklyn Botanic Garden, 1000 Washington Ave., Brooklyn, NY 11225.

An unusual but useful bulletin is *Ornamental Grasses for the Home and Garden.* This can be ordered for 30¢ from:

Mailing Room, Bldg. 7, Research Park, Cornell University, Ithaca, NY 14850.

The New Wave. Here is a list of landscape books that focus on natural and edible landscaping:

Rosalind Creasy, *The Complete Book of Edible Landscaping.* San Francisco: Sierra Club Books, 1982. An extraordinary book by a landscape architect with an unusually broad knowledge of plants. It covers the use of edible plants in hedges, as groundcovers, and in borders, and includes imaginative and delightful landscaping plans, recipes, ecological information, conservation practices, and much more.

John Dickelmann and Robert Schuster, *Natural Landscaping: Designing with Native Plant Communities.* New York: McGraw-Hill, 1982. This study is aimed at the northeast area of this country and southern Canada.

Verandas, porches of commodious dimensions, summer houses, arbors, garden retreats, and grottoes were all part of the peaceful and beautiful landscaped gardens of our great-grandparents. Here is a "Chinese temple" garden structure with a view of the water.

It urges observation of a natural "model" to the reader and is particularly good in showing how to analyze your site.

Anne Simon Moffat and Marc Schiler, *Landscape Designs That Save Energy.* New York: William Morrow, 1981. An unusual and provocative book that deserves a good look before you start transplanting.

Carol A. Smyser and the editors of Rodale Press Books, *Nature's Design: A Practical Guide to Natural Landscaping.* Emmaus, Pa: Rodale Press, 1982. A very detailed guide to natural landscaping, covering diverse ecological regions and small suburban plots as well as rolling acres. The site planning charts are outstanding.

You can use the pages that follow to diagram the locations of all the permanent planting areas on your property. Indicate the position of the vegetable garden, herb and flower gardens, and berry patches, and also the locations of individual fruit trees and ornamental trees and shrubs. And don't forget to show the location of your house and any outbuildings you have. Refer to these diagrams whenever you're considering adding new garden areas to your home landscape.

Basic Landscape Plans

Perennials

Perennials have become immensely popular in the last few years, but probably no other branch of gardening takes such careful planning, wide correspondence, and good record-keeping as growing perennials. Before you start filling out order blanks, know that successful perennial beds and garden borders are a test of your gardening skill. The great English garden writers produced a classic body of books on perennial gardening, but many of these have become scarce or rare; Gertrude Jekyll's famous 1908 work, *Color in the Flower Garden,* fetches hundreds of dollars if you can find a copy. Horticultural libraries (see the listing on page 71) are marvelous places to spend a rainy day and allow you to see and use rare books otherwise out of your reach. There is much to be learned from the past. But there are also excellent modern guides to planning perennial borders and growing these long-lived plants. Here are a few:

Robert S. Hebb, *Low Maintenance Perennials.* Arnold Arboretum, 1975.

Perennials for Low Maintenance Gardening; Arnoldia, Jan., Mar., May, 1971. Order all four from The Arnold Arboretum, Jamaica Plain, MA 02130.

The Brooklyn Botanic Garden handbook series includes the following of interest to perennial gardeners: No. 25, *100 Finest Trees and Shrubs;* No. 56, *Summer Flowers for Continuing Bloom;* No. 83, *Nursery Source Guide;* and No. 87, *Perennials and Their Uses.* Each costs $2.85 and may be ordered from:

Brooklyn Botanic Garden, 1000 Washington Ave., Brooklyn, NY 11225.

If you have a small space and still long to grow perennials, see *Perennial Flowers for Small Gardens,* Pan Piper Series. This can be ordered for $2.50 from:

Walt Nicke, Box 71, Hudson, NY 12534.

Gardeners planning perennial borders are interested in color masses and continuous bloom as well as plants that will do well in their climate. Scores of books on perennial gardening list flowers by color for the reader's ease in choosing plants for border layouts and design. A useful bulletin is New York State Extension Bulletin 1190, *Sequence of Bloom of Perennials, Biennials and Bulbs.* The bulletin is free to New York State residents, 25¢ to out-of-staters. Order from:

Publications, Cooperative Extension Service, N.Y. State College of Agriculture, Cornell University, Ithaca, NY 14850.

A widely used color chart gardeners employ to work out perennial planting designs is the Negs Fisher Color Chart. This can be ordered from:

Charles T. Basle, 11 Rockridge Rd., Waltham, MA 02154.

Very useful to serious gardeners is the concise bibli-

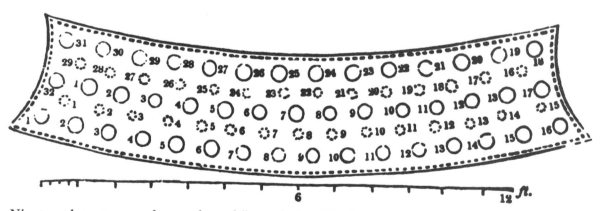

Nineteenth-century gardeners planned flower beds with minute attention to detail as well as for stunning effects. Here is a paper plan for a flower bed of plants in many varieties with red flowers only. The plants are set out in such a manner that equal numbers bloom from April until frost, providing at least seven months of continuous crimson.

ography of books on perennial gardening in Thomas and Betty Powell's *The Avant Gardener* (Boston: Houghton Mifflin Co., 1975). The same authors put out an informative grab-bag horticultural newsletter by the same name—*The Avant Gardener.* Especially interesting is vol. 14, no. 8 (June, 1982), a special review of perennials by Pamela J. Harper, a well-known garden photographer and plant expert. Special reprints may be ordered at $1.50 from:

Thomas and Betty Powell, *The Avant Gardener,* Horticultural Data Processors, Box 489, New York, NY 10028.

Here is a concise list of plantsmen specializing in perennials:

East

White Flower Farm, Litchfield, CT 06759.

Lounsberry Gardens, Box 135, Oakford, IL 62673.

Conley's Garden Center, Boothbay Harbor, ME 04538.

Daystar, RFD #2, Litchfield, ME 04350.

The Rock Garden, Litchfield, ME 04350.

Tranquil Lake Nursery, 45 River St., Rehoboth, MA 02769.

We-Du Nurseries, 21 Worley St., West Roxbury, MA 02132.

Rakestraw's Gardens, 3094 S. Term St., Burton, MI 48529.

Far North Gardens, 15621 Auburndale Ave., Livonia, MI 48154.

Busse Garden Center, 635 E. 7th St., Cokato, MN 55321.

Holbrook Farm and Nursery, Rt. 2, Box 223B, Fletcher, NC 28732.

Powell's Gardens, Rt. 2, Hwy. 70, Princeton, NC 27569.

Rocknoll Nursery, 9210 U.S. 50, Hillsboro, OH 45133.

Bluestone Perennials, 7211 Middle Ridge Rd., Madison, OH 44057.

Garden Place, 6780 Heisley Rd., Mentor, OH 44060.

Appalachian Wildflower Nursery, Rt. 1, Box 275A, Reedsville, PA 17084.

Woodlanders, Inc., 1128 Colleton Ave., Aiken, SC 29801.

Wayside Gardens, Hodges, SC 29695.

Andre Viette Farm & Nursery, Rt. 1, Box 16, Fisherville, VA 22939.

Milaeger's Gardens, 4838 Douglas Ave., Racine, WI 53402.

West

Pacific Bamboo Gardens, 4754 Vista La., San Diego, CA 92116.

Melrose Gardens, 209 Best Rd. S, Stockton, CA 95205.

Plants of the Southwest, 1570 Pacheco St., Santa Fe, NM 87501.

Nature's Garden, Rt. 1, Box 488, Beaverton, OR 97007.

Siskiyou Rare Plant Nursery, 2825 Cummings Rd., Medford, OR 97501.

Russell Graham, 4030 Eashle Crest Rd. NW, Salem, OR 97304.

Laurie's Garden, 1886 McKenzie Hwy., Springfield, OR 97477.

The Wild Garden, Box 487, Bothell, WA 98011.

Lamb Nurseries, E. 101 Sharp Ave., Spokane, WA 99202.

The following pages are for cultural records on the performance of your perennials and for detailed plans of what's planted where in the perennial beds and borders.

Perennial Plants Record

Species & Cultivar	Source	Date Planted	Cost	Cultural Notes

Species & Cultivar	Source	Date Planted	Cost	Cultural Notes

Perennial Beds & Borders Plans

Ornamental Trees and Shrubs

Information on tree care, layout planning, casualty losses, and legal matters comes from experts allied with the American Society of Consulting Arborists. For a membership list of tree experts in the United States and Canada, write:

American Society of Consulting Arborists, 12 Lakeview Ave., Milltown, NJ 08850.

Growing trees from seed can be an absorbing hobby. Here are two sources of tree seed:

Herbst Brothers Seedsmen, Inc., 1000 N. Main St., Brewster, NY 10509. Their wholesale catalog lists an excellent variety of seeds.

F. W. Schumacher, Sandwich, MA 02563.

Help in growing trees from seed is found in Cornell Extension Bulletin 1198, *Growing Trees in Small Nurseries.* Order from:

Mailing Room, Bldg. 7, Research Park, Cornell University, Ithaca, NY 14850.

USDA Miscellaneous Publication No. 654, *Woody Plant Seed Manual,* is an outstanding guide to tree-seed growing. Order from:

Superintendent of Documents, U.S. Government Printing Office, Washington, DC 20402. The price is $4.

Several nurseries specialize in the newer shade and flowering trees developed by plant breeders. Arboretums and botanic gardens are excellent places to visit and examine growing tree specimens that are suitable for your region before you fill out nursery orders. Write for the tree catalogs of these nurseries:

Monrovia Nursery, Azusa, CA 91702.

Saratoga Horticultural Foundation, Box 108, Saratoga, CA 95070.

Princeton Nurseries, Princeton, NJ 08540.

Cole Nursery Co., R.D. 1, Circleville, OH 43113.

E. H. Scanlon & Associates, 7621 Lewis Rd., Olmstead Falls, OH 44138.

You can use the space on the next two pages to keep track of the performance of your ornamental trees and shrubs. Their locations on your property can be recorded on the basic landscape plans on pages 28 to 31.

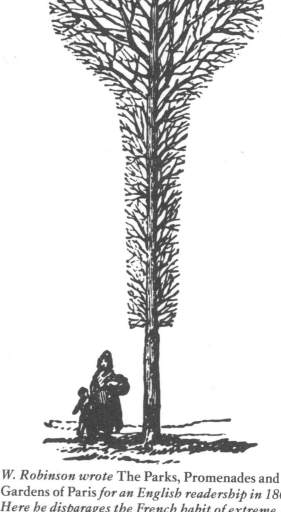

W. Robinson wrote The Parks, Promenades and Gardens of Paris *for an English readership in 1869. Here he disparages the French habit of extreme tree pruning. "The lamentable effect of clipping the trees is well shown in the plate; it is very evident the poor trees do not like it. It would be difficult to find a more striking example of labour worse than thrown away than that bestowed on clipping trees in many French gardens."*

Trees and Shrubs Record

Species & Cultivar	Source	Date Planted	Cost	Cultural Notes

Species & Cultivar	Source	Date Planted	Cost	Cultural Notes

Bulbs

Bulbs draw many gardeners like magnets, and there are certainly enough kinds to choose among—hyacinths, alliums, tuberous begonias, elatior begonias, tulips, camassias, fritillarias, Bengal lilies, crocosmias, crocuses, dahlias, daffodils, erythroniums, freesias, gladioli, irises, snowflakes, and many lilies. Nearly every seed and plant house carries a selection of bulbs, but some dealers specialize in bulbs and offer intriguing rarities. Following is a list of a few of the dozens of bulb sellers. Firms that specialize in a particular area are noted; the others have more diversified selections of bulbs.

Van Engelen Inc., Box 11, Stamford, CT 06904.

Tranquil Lake Nursery, 45 River St., Rehoboth, MA 02769.

P. De Jaeger & Sons, South Hamilton, MA 01982.

International Growers' Exchange, Box 397, Farmington, MI 48024.

John Scheepers, Inc., 63-65 Wall St., New York, NY 10005.

The Thompsons, P.O. Drawer PP, Southampton, NY 11968. Begonias.

Rex Bulb Farms, Newburg, OR 97132.

Wayside Gardens, Hodges, SC 29695.

Mary Mattison Van Schaik, Cavendish, VT 05142. Old favorites.

Lamb Nurseries, E. 101 Sharp Ave., Spokane, WA 99202.

Specialized cultural information is available from suppliers, but a good starter book is:

Patrick Synge, *The Complete Guide to Bulbs.* New York: Dutton, n.d.

The pages that follow will help you to keep tabs on bulb purchases, plantings, and performance, as well as the locations of bulbs in beds and naturalized plantings on your property.

A bulb case for forcing bulbs indoors. Each bulb is set in a dark jar of rainwater, which is changed weekly. After bloom the bulbs are set out in the garden to "strengthen" and "preserve" them. Such plant furniture was common a century ago but has been replaced today by small and dismal pots.

Bulb Record

Species & Cultivar	Source	Cost	Date Planted	Date Separated	Cultural Notes
Tulips					

Species & Cultivar	Source	Cost	Date Planted	Date Separated	Cultural Notes

Species & Cultivar	Source	Cost	Date Planted	Date Separated	Cultural Notes

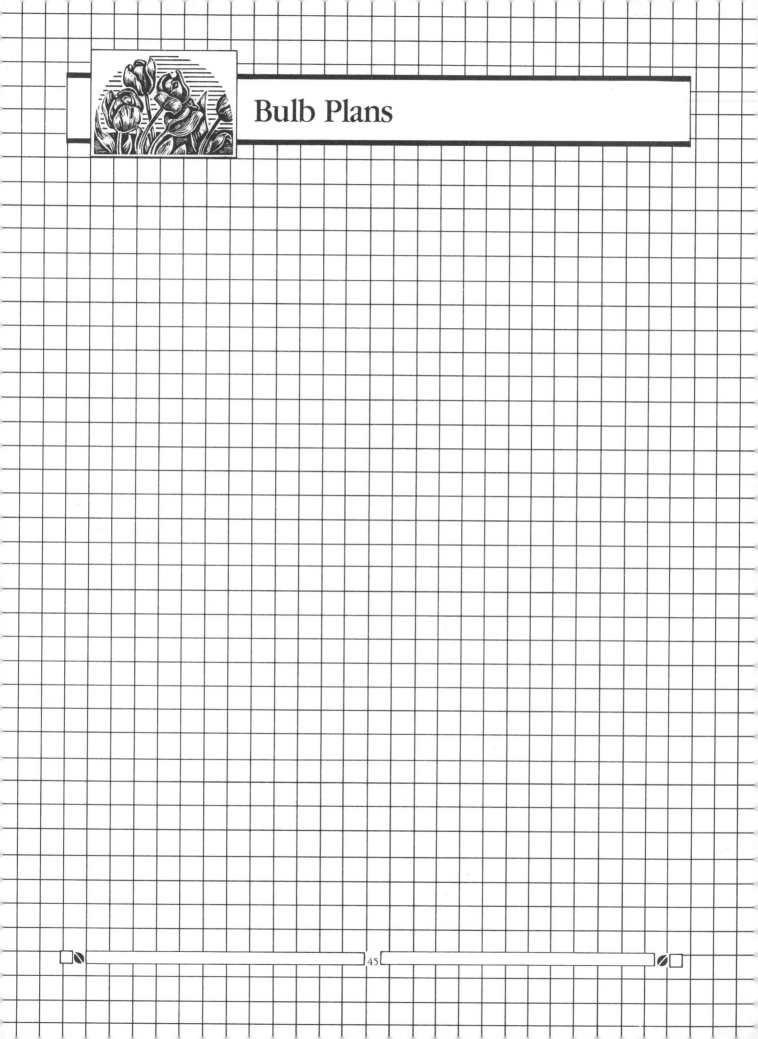

Bulb Plans

Rose Gardens, Herb Gardens, and Other Gardens

If you have always longed for a rose garden but fear the hit-or-miss look of an unplanned rose collection, start by asking advice from:

The American Rose Society, Box 30,000, Shreveport, LA 71130. This national organization can direct you to your local rose society, advise on cultivars and cultural techniques, and much more. The society publishes *American Rose Magazine* and offers a *Handbook for Selecting Roses,* an annual, and a free rose bush for annual dues of $18.

Some sources of roses include:

Armstrong Nurseries, Box 473, Ontario, CA 91764.

Tillotson's Roses, Brown's Valley Rd., Watsonville, CA 95076.

Joseph J. Kern Rose Nursery, Box 33, Mentor, OH 44060.

Jackson & Perkins Co., Medford, OR 97501.

Roses by Fred Edmunds, Box 68, Wilsonville, OR 97070.

Herb Gardens. Growing and designing herb gardens has become a gardening rage. The uses of herbs—culinary, medicinal, for fragrant potpourris and tussy-mussys— have an ancient and dignified history. Whether your herb garden is a tiny, sunny corner outside the kitchen door or an elaborate knot garden, you will be rewarded by following up some of the following herb sources.

There are scores of books about herbs, and among the most interesting are the following:

Gertrude B. Foster and Rosemary F. Louden, *Park's Success with Herbs.* Greenwood, S.C.: Geo. W. Park Seed Co., 1980. The best book on growing herbs.

Maurice Messegue, *Of Men and Plants.* New York: Macmillan, 1973. The English translation of the classic French medicinal herbal.

A rich source of information on herbs and herb gardens is:

The Herb Society of America, Horticultural Hall, 300 Massachusetts Ave., Boston, MA 02115.

Periodicals devoted to herbs and reviewing outstanding herb gardens are:

Herb Growers Magazine, Herb Grower Press, Falls Village, CT 06031.

The Herb Quarterly, West St., Newfane, VT 05345.

Whitchappel's Herbal, Box 272, Peterborough, NH 03458.

Other Gardens. Hundreds of specialized plantings are possible to suit the gardening tastes of all regions. You may wish to plan an oriental vegetable plot, a rock garden, or a series of plots for small grains or concentrate on water plants, cacti, or tropical exotics. Pages 56 to 59 will accommodate cultural records and plans for some special gardens.

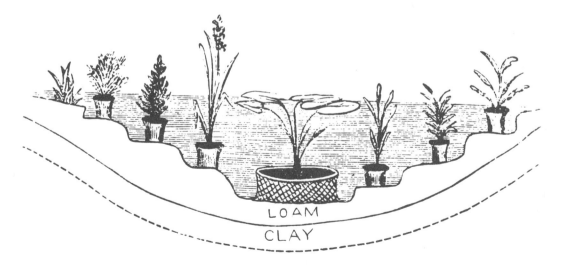

A plan for a water garden, very popular in gardens of yesteryear.

Rose Records

Species & Cultivar	Source	Date Planted	Cultural Notes	Propagation Notes

Species & Cultivar	Source	Date Planted	Cultural Notes	Propagation Notes

Rose Garden Plans

Herb Record

Species & Cultivar	Source	Date Planted	Cultural Notes	Propagation	Uses

Species & Cultivar	Source	Date Planted	Cultural Notes	Propagation	Uses

Herb Garden Plans

_____ Record

Species & Cultivar	Source	Date Planted	Cultural Notes	Propagation

Species & Cultivar	Source	Date Planted	Cultural Notes	Propagation

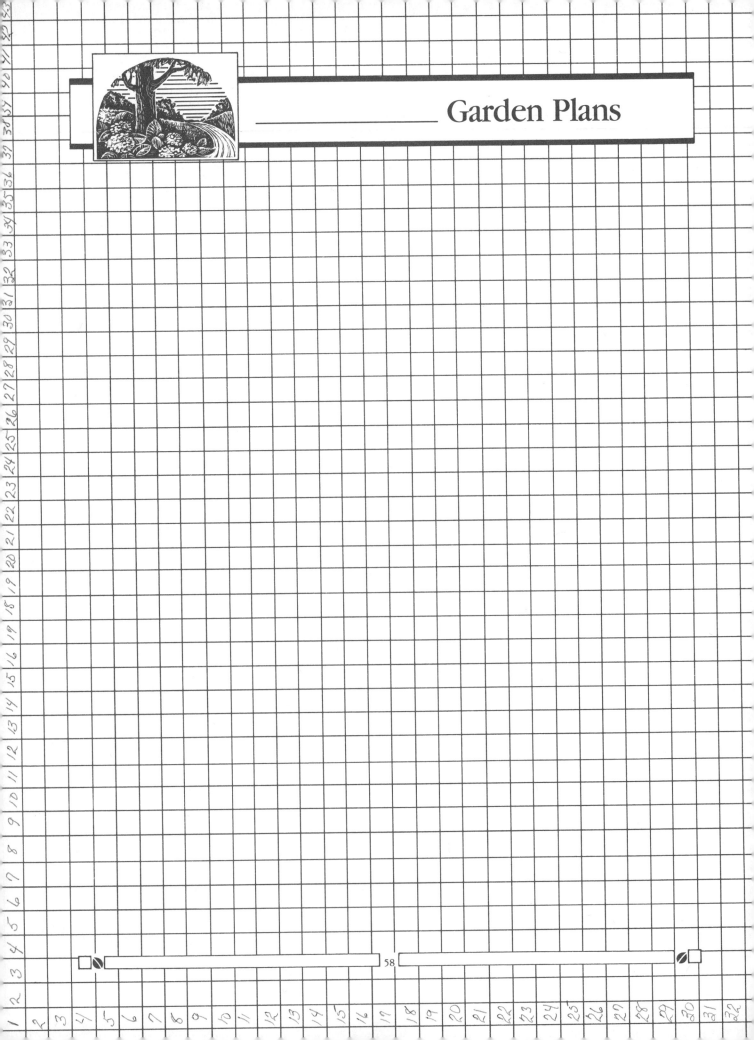

Garden Plans

Compost and Fertilizers

What Plants Need

Plants need 16 elements to grow and develop properly. Three basics, carbon, hydrogen, and oxygen, they draw from water and the atmosphere. Three others—sometimes called the primary nutrients—are nitrogen, phosphorus, and potassium, and frequently there are not enough of these elements present in garden soil to nourish plants. The secondary nutrients—calcium, magnesium, and sulfur—may be deficient in an exhausted or poor soil. The vital micronutrients— boron, copper, iron, manganese, molybdenum, zinc, and chlorine—must be present for the plant's physiological processes. The availability of the nutrients to a plant's roots depends on the soil pH: too acid a soil can lock up nitrogen, phosphorus, calcium, sulfur, potassium, magnesium, and molybdenum; too alkaline a soil can make iron, boron, manganese, copper, and zinc difficult for the plants to get.

When soil test results or plant growth and development observations show that nutrients are locked up or deficient in soil, you can supply the plants by adding fertilizers or liming acid soil to bring up the pH. Organic fertilizers such as animal manures, green manure crops, and compost not only replenish the nutrient supply, but improve soil structure and tilth.

Compost

Compost is nothing more than organic materials that have been piled up and allowed to decompose to a crumbly, soil-like material that can be worked into the garden soil. Leaves, immature weeds, kitchen vegetable scraps, grass clippings, manure, sawdust, straw, apple and grape pomace, seaweed, and many other waste materials have their places in the compost pile. A compost pile—contained in a bin or enclosure which allows air to supply oxygen to the mass—is built up in layers of rough plant materials, green vegetation, and kitchen waste, and an occasional layer of soil and animal manure if it's available. The pile must be kept damp to spur on the aerobic microbiotic life teeming in the pile.

A good time to start the compost pile is with spring

What Doesn't Go in the Compost Pile

Avoid the following material in your compost pile:
1. Diseased plants or cuttings bearing insect eggs and cases;
2. Mature weeds whose seeds may survive the pile's heat, ivy, bindweed, Bermuda grass, cockleburs, and burdock burrs;
3. Poisonous plant material—castor bean, oleander, poison ivy, and others;
4. Human, cat, or dog manures, which can have pathogens that escape the pile's heat.

cleanup. Add to the pile during the summer with whatever compostable material comes to hand. In the fall add garden wastes and leaves. By garden time the next spring, the pile is probably ready to be used in the garden as mulch if it is still fairly bulky, or, if it has decomposed to a crumbly, fine-textured material, worked into the soil. Many fast compost heaps are ready to use a few months after they are started.

Here are two recipes for making compost. A simple outdoor heap can be made by combining equal parts of leaves, fresh grass clippings, and horse manure, and adding a liberal sprinkling of rock powders. For faster compost, shred the ingredients before mixing them together. Apartment dwellers and others who want to make compost in small amounts can try writer and organic gardener Vic Sussman's method of indoor composting. In a 5-gallon can that has a lid, alternate layers of fresh kitchen scraps (vegetable peelings, coffee grounds, and other non-meat wastes) that have been pureed in a blender, with layers of sawdust an inch or more deep. Keep repeating layers until the can is full, ending with a layer of sawdust. Stir every day until the compost is ready.

Bag Composting. Even suburban and urban gardeners can have compost heaps. Take a plastic 32-gallon leaf bag, fill it with layers of grass clippings, leaves, an occasional sprinkle of lime and fertilizer, dampen the whole mass with a quart of water, tie it up tightly, and store it in a cellar or heated garage over the winter. It will yield a nice bagful of rich, crumbly compost the next spring.

Over-Winter Composting. Cold-climate gardeners can keep some activity going in their compost piles by insulating the pile with hay bales and covering the top with a window sash facing south to catch the sun.

There are numerous other composting recipes and procedures, and you can read about them in various books, including:

Alice Heckel, ed., *The Pfeiffer Garden Book.* Stroudsburg, Pa.: Biodynamic Farming and Gardening Association, 1967. Describes the biodynamic method of composting, which uses no manure or nitrogen supplements.

John Jeavons, *How to Grow More Vegetables.* Berkeley, Calif.: Ten Speed Press, 1979. Also discusses

---

2795. *Practical limit to ingredients for composts.* Cushing, one of the best writers on the propagation of exotics, observes, " Loam, peat, and sand seem to be the three simples of nature, if I may so call them, most requisite for our purpose ; to which we occasionally add, as mollifiers, vegetable or leaf mould, and well-rotted dung; from the judicious mixture and preparation of which, composts may be made to suit plants introduced from any quarter of the globe." (*Exotic Gardener,* p. 153. 1814.) Sweet (*Botanical Cultivator,* 1820) concurs in this opinion. See also Haynes *On Collecting and Forming Composts,* &c., 1821.

2796. *Preparation of composts.* The preparation requisite for the heavy and light composts for general enrichment, and of the above different earths, consists in collecting each sort in the compost-ground, in separate ridges of three or four feet broad and as many high, and turning them every six weeks or two months for a year, or a year and a half, before they are used. Peat earth or heath earth, being generally procured in the state of turves full of the roots and tops of heath, requires two or three years to rot ; but, after it has lain one year, it may be sifted, and what passes through a small sieve will be found fit for use. Some nurserymen use both these loams and peats as soon as procured, and find them answer perfectly for most plants ; but for delicate flowers, and especially bulbs, and all florists' flowers, and for all composts into the composition of which manures enter, not less than one year ought to be allowed for decomposition, and what is technically called sweetening. The French gardeners allow for their rich orange-tree composts from three to six years.

This section on composting from J. C. Loudon's famous An Encyclopedia of Gardening *(published in London in 1835) shows that composting was common practice 150 years ago.*

biodynamic composting.

Jerry Minnich, Marjorie Hunt, and the editors of *Organic Gardening* magazine, *The Rodale Guide to Composting.* Emmaus, Pa.: Rodale Press, 1979. Contains clear, detailed explanations of the biological and chemical processes involved in composting, explains various methods of constructing a heap, and provides instructions for custom-making compost for individual gardens.

Staff of *Organic Gardening* magazine, ed., *The Encyclopedia of Organic Gardening.* Emmaus, Pa.: Rodale Press, 1978. Gives capsule descriptions of the most popular methods, along with charts of materials to use in compost.

Vic Sussman, *Easy Composting.* Emmaus, Pa.: Rodale Press, 1982. A briefer, less technical treatment, with a good explanation of how compost works and a review of options for composting.

The following page can be used for keeping a record of compost you make by different methods and with varying ingredients. You may find, for example, that you come to prefer one compost blend for flowering perennials and a different blend for the vegetable garden.

Cover Crops

Experienced gardeners know that letting a bare dirt garden lie fallow after harvest is not the best thing to do. The ancient practice of green manures—crops grown deliberately to be turned into the soil—will help make soil nutrients available to crop plants, add nitrogen to the soil, prevent wind and water erosion, halt compacting of the soil, improve tilth, provide a superb natural environment for earthworms and microorganic life, and a good deal more. Buckwheat, ryegrass, legumes, clovers, kale, beans, and peas have all been used as cover crops, as have hairy indigo, smooth brome-grass, lespedeza, millet, and even weeds. Although most gardening books and encyclopedias have brief sections on green manures, and agricultural bulletins advise useful cover crops for particular sections of the country and for certain purposes, two very good guides are published by Garden Way Publishing Co., Charlotte, VT 05445. The bulletin, *Cover Crop Gardening, Soil Enrichment with Green Manures,* is a concise 31-page guide to cover crops, and Richard Alther and Richard Raymond's *Improving Garden Soil with Green Manures,* 1974, is extremely helpful.

The space on page 64 will help you to keep track of cover crop plantings—which green manure crops are planted where, dates of planting and turning under, and how effective the plantings seem to be.

Horse Manure—An Overlooked Resource

Almost every gardener regards cow manure as brown gold, far superior to every other kind of animal manure. But horse manure really makes the garden grow. Fresh horse manure is roughly 25 to 30 percent richer in nutrients than cow manure. It is made up of two-thirds solid manure, one-fourth bedding, and one-sixth liquid. It contains more plant food than cow manure, and, because of its looser texture, decomposes more rapidly. Fresh horse manure applied to heavy clay soils can significantly improve the drainage and tilth of the soil. If you live in an area where there are horse stables or racetracks, ask about taking away the manure—it's the best you can get.

Compost

Method	Pile Started	Pile Finished	Yield	Results

Cover Crops

Cover Crop	Date Sown	Place Sown	Date Turned Under	Comments

Fertilizers and Manures

Fertilizer Type	Age & Condition	Place Applied	Date	Comments

Techniques and Resources

For a long time the only way to garden in this country was in long, weedless rows of the same vegetable widely spaced, with plenty of bare soil showing. Many older gardeners still like to see bare ground in the garden. But the garden revolution of the past two decades has shown us how to get fantastic yields from small gardens; how to grow plants where there is no open ground at all; how to extend short seasons; how to use mulches, cloches, and windbreaks; and natural procedures to condition and enrich the soil. Here is a brief review of some of the major new techniques and sources of information and expertise that may tempt you into experimental and exciting new ways of gardening.

Organic Gardening

The organic method of gardening is linked with the work of British agronomist Sir Albert Howard, whose book, *An Agricultural Testament,* appeared in 1940. In this country, Sir Howard's ideas were popularized by J. I. Rodale. Today, organic gardening, which uses organic material instead of chemicals to condition soil, to keep the natural beneficial microbial action in the soil lively, and to provide nutrients for plants, is widely practiced. In the 40 years the organic movement has been around, it has progressed from the backyard gardens of a few "cranks" to a commonly accepted way of gardening, is practiced in

university and experimental station fields, and is now even used in a few areas by commercial agriculturists.

Rodale Press in Emmaus, Pennsylvania, remains an important source of information and literature on organic gardening techniques. The periodical *Organic Gardening* is read monthly by more than a million gardeners.

Organic Gardening Subscriptions, 33 E. Minor St., Emmaus, PA 18049. A subscription costs $11 annually.

An important organization for organic gardeners and farmers is the Natural Organic Farmers Association (NOFA), which publishes a newsletter and holds a famous three-day annual conference with hundreds of workshops and lectures by experts in all branches of gardening, farming, and agricultural skills. For information on membership and the annual conference, write:

NOFA, Box 335, Antrim, NH 03440.

High-Density Planting

The old row style of gardening wastes a tremendous amount of garden area. Bed or wide row plantings are 4 to 5 feet wide and any length you find convenient. Plants are set in a diagonal pattern for maximum use of the space. Nurseries and commercial growers have been quick to see the economic advantage of bed plantings that increase yields three to four times over that of row planting.

Raised Beds. These provide better drainage than level beds, suffer no ill effects from soil compaction, and are easy to work in. They can be as simple as beds of soil and organic material heaped 6 to 8 inches higher than the garden level or as elaborate as deep beds of several feet enclosed in stone walls or stacked railroad ties.

The Biodynamic French Intensive Method. This method of gardening uses raised or deep beds that have 24-inch depths of soil improved with organic matter for spectacular results. One of the best explanations of this gardening method is found in John Jeavons' *How to Grow More Vegetables.* Another outstanding presentation of this method (where it is called deep bed gardening) is John Seymour's *The Self-Sufficient Gardener: A Complete Guide to Growing and Preserving All Your Own Food* (New York: Doubleday & Co., 1979).

Double-Digging. This is an arduous but worthwhile way of preparing a wide bed 2 feet deep, a task that is integral to the Biodynamic French Intensive method. It is still a favored practice in England, that country of expert gardeners. First, compost and manure are spread over the area to be double-dug, then the topsoil and compost layer is removed to a depth of 1 foot the length of the trench.

This material is set aside. The exposed subsoil is then loosened and aerated with a spade or fork to a depth of 1 foot. Next, the topsoil and compost layer of an adjoining trench is removed and tossed into the first trench, where it lies atop the loosened subsoil. The subsoil in the second trench is spaded loose to a depth of 1 foot, just as was done with the first trench. Finally, the topsoil and compost that was set aside from the first trench is shoveled into the second trench. Voila! a double-dug bed is ready.

Mulch

The late Ruth Stout (author of *How to Have a Green Thumb without an Aching Back,* New York: Cornerstone, 1968 and *Gardening without Work,* New York: Cornerstone, 1974) made mulching a well-known gardening technique. Mulch is a layer of organic or nonorganic material spread through the garden and around plants. Different results and techniques are associated with the various mulching mediums. Favorites include aluminum foil; clear, black, blue, and green plastic films; a new biodegradable plastic; and many organic materials, such as old alfalfa hay, buckwheat hulls, cocoa bean hulls, shredded cornstalks, salt hay, sawdust, straw, bark, and more.

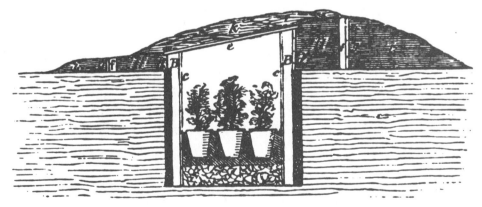

Copeland's Country Life: A Handbook of Agriculture, Horticulture, and Landscape Gardening *(published in Boston in 1859) is packed with wonderful designs and plans of interest to gardeners. Here is a cold pit for wintering over potted plants. The pit is sited in a place sheltered from the prevailing winter wind, on level ground but with good drainage. The pit is insulated with shredded bark and lined with boards. It has a glass cover, which, when winter is about to set in, is covered 6 inches deep with leaves or straw and then again with a layer of boards. In the spring the coverings were gradually removed, and the glass cover helped the cold pit become a warm, sheltered atmosphere ideal for revitalizing plants.*

The advantages of mulching are that the soil retains moisture in a dry year; soil temperatures are steady; the soil is protected from compacting by heavy rain or foot traffic; earthworms flourish under the mulch; and, if organic mulches are used, the soil is conditioned and enriched as the mulch breaks down.

The disadvantages of mulching are that, in a wet year, mulching can encourage fungus diseases and reduce the oxygen supply to plants; acid mulches such as softwood sawdust and pine needles have restricted uses; fresh green mulching materials will draw nitrogen from the soil as they decompose; and snails and slugs enjoy the cool, damp environment under the mulch.

Nearly every gardening book now carries a detailed section on mulching techniques and materials. An important article on leaf mulching is found in No. 7 of the *Journal of New Alchemists.* The Brooklyn Botanic Garden Handbook No. 23, *Mulches,* can be ordered from the Brooklyn Botanic Garden, 1000 Washington Ave., Brooklyn, NY 11225.

Ring Culture

This space-saving technique combining soil and soilless culture was developed several decades ago at Tilgate Horticultural Research Station in England. Bottomless cylinders are set on a base of gravel or boiler ash and filled with a rich soil mix. The plants are grown in the cylinders. The roots extend prodigiously into the lower gravel layer. The yields from this technique of growing plants are very high, and the method is favored for tomato growing, inside or outside the greenhouse. The procedure is described in detail in Frank Allerton's *Ring Culture* (London: Faber & Faber, 1972).

Bag Gardens

Drs. Richard Sheldrake and J. W. Boodley of Cornell University developed this high yield "Pillow Pak" technique which gives would-be gardeners in cities a chance to grow terrific vegetables on balconies or on paved areas. Dark polyethylene bags are filled with a sterile, soilless mix, and are stood upright. The plants grow through slits cut in the bags, and nourishment comes from a fertilizer-tea formula. The bags and instructions for bag growing can be ordered from: Plant 'N Bags, W. R. Grace and Co., 62 Whittemore Ave., Cambridge, MA 02140.

Container Gardening

One of the most explosively popular gardening techniques in the last decade has been growing plants—from trees to vegetables and flowers—in containers, including tubs, pots, window boxes, bushel baskets, hanging planters, and barrels. There are several useful books on the subject, such as the following:

Brooklyn Botanic Garden Handbook No. 85, *Container Gardening,* 1978.

Jack Kramer, *Hanging Gardens: Basket Plants Indoors and Out.* New York: Charles Scribner's Sons, 1971.

_____, *Container Gardening Indoors and Out.* New York: Doubleday, n.d.

George Taloumis, *Outdoor Gardening in Pots and Boxes.* New York: Van Nostrand Reinhold Co., n.d.

Henry Teuscher, *Window Box Gardening.* New York: Macmillan, 1956.

Espalier and Ornamental Pruning

Espaliered pear trees against a garden wall are a magnificent sight and demonstrate considerable horticultural skill. All sorts of plants are being espaliered now in the recent revival of this medieval technique. If you would like to try your hand at it, the best introduction to the art is Harold O. Perkins, *Espaliers and Vines for the Home Gardener* (New York: Van Nostrand Reinhold Co., 1979). Espaliering and other methods of ornamental pruning—pollarding, topiary, and pleaching—are covered in the Brooklyn Botanic Garden Handbook No. 36, *Trained and Sculptured Plants.*

Dwarf fruit trees already espalier-trained in a number of patterns and shapes can be ordered from:

Henry Leuthardt Nurseries, Inc., E. Moriches, Long Island, NY 11940.

Bonsai

The Brooklyn Botanic Garden has a superb collection of bonsai and an outstanding collection of books on the subject in the library and Garden Shop, and offers classes in bonsai as well as a series of handbooks that take the interested gardener from the beginning to advanced bonsai work. See Handbooks No. 13, *Dwarfed Potted Trees: The Bonsai of Japan;* No. 37, *Japanese Gardens and Miniature Landscapes;* No. 51, *Bonsai: Special Techniques;* and No. 81, *Bonsai for Indoors.*

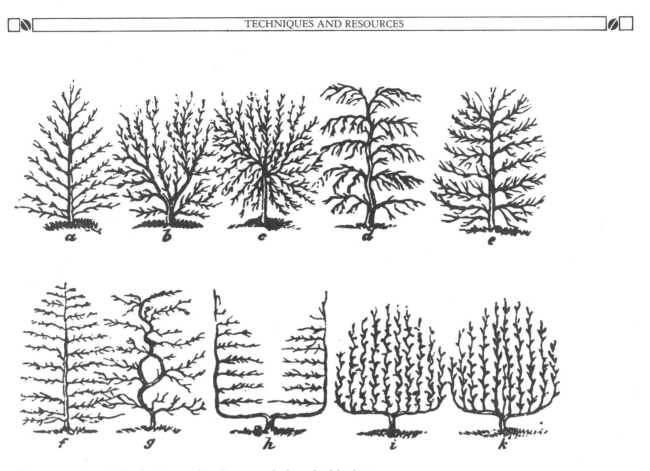

Here are a few of the basic espalier forms so beloved of fruit-tree growers in the last century: a, *herringbone fan;* b, *irregular fan;* c, *stellate fan;* d, *drooping fan;* e, *wavy fan;* f, *horizontal;* g, *horizontal with screw stem;* h, *horizontal with double stem;* i, *vertical with screw shoots;* j, *vertical with upright shoots.*

Learning More

Correspondence courses in horticultural techniques, soils, fruit growing, garden design and landscaping, vegetable growing, entomology, lawns, pruning, and other subjects are available from a number of universities and associations. Most home study courses include cassette tapes and slides as well as textbooks. A planned program of courses can lead to a degree in horticulture or agriculture through most of the schools listed below. A single course in a field of special interest to you is a wonderful way to pass the winter. Write for catalogs to help you make a choice.

Department of Correspondence Study, 805 Seagle Bldg., University of Florida, Gainesville, FL 32601.

Independent Study Program, 202 Agricultural Education Bldg., Pennsylvania State University, University Park, PA 16802.

Independent Study Program, Extension Service, Utah State University, Logan, UT 84321.

Independent Study Program, Brigham Young University, Provo, UT 84601.

Home Study Program, National Arborist Association, 1750 Old Meadow Rd., McLean, VA 22101.

Bureau of Correspondence Courses, General Extension Service, Washington State University, Pullman, WA 99163.

Independent Study, Office of Continuing Education, University of Guelph, Guelph, ON N1G 2W1, Canada.

An intensive 19-month program of professional horticultural training is available at:

The New York Botanical Garden School of Horticulture, New York Botanical Garden, Bronx, NY 10458.

Horticultural and Garden Societies

Many states have state horticultural societies and garden clubs. Municipal and other regional garden organizations abound. A tremendous amount of information and news is available through the publications and newsletters of various societies. Local affiliated groups are listed, and often special travel tours or unusual offerings in plant materials are available to members. Write for membership applications.

American Horticultural Society, 910 Washington St., Alexandria, VA 22314.

Garden Club of America, 598 Madison Ave., New York, NY 10022.

Men's Garden Club of America, 5560 Merle Hay Rd., Des Moines, IA 50323.

National Council of State Garden Clubs, 4401 Magnolia Ave., St. Louis, MO 63110.

Massachusetts Horticultural Society, 300 Massachusetts Ave., Boston, MA 02115.

Pennsylvania Horticultural Society, 325 Walnut St., Philadelphia, PA 19106.

Plant Societies

Plant societies are for specialty gardeners and offer new information in the field; correspondence with other gardeners keen on the same plants; news of special offerings, shows, and exhibitions; classes, tours, and bulletins or periodicals; as well as expert advice. Beginner, connoisseur, master gardener—all can benefit from membership in plant societies.

The addresses of many of the societies change with the officers, so contact your nearest horticultural society for the current address of the group you're interested in. Here are some of the plant societies that exist: American Amaryllis Society, American Begonia Society, American Bonsai Society, Inc., American Boxwood Society, American Camellia Society, American Daffodil Society, American Dahlia Society, American Fern Society, American Fuchsia Society, American Gloxinia and Gesneriad Society, American Hemerocallis Society, American Hibiscus Society, American Hosta Society, American Iris Society, American Magnolia Society, American Orchid Society, American Primrose Society, American Rhododendron Society, American Rock Garden Society, American Rose Society, Bromeliad Society, Cactus and Succulent Society of America, Epiphyllum Society, Herb

The extraordinary container for this **Gymnostachyum verschaffeltii** *was considered* très chic *in last century's Paris, where great pots and tubs of plants were on display in public places and private houses in large quantity.*

Society of America, Indoor Light Gardening Society of America, International Geranium Society, National Oleander Society, North American Gladiolus Society, The Palm Society, and Saintpaulia International. There are lots of other groups too, and many have local chapters wherever there are enough members.

Fruit Growers' Associations

These associations are often sources of heirloom or rare plant material and inform members of new cultural techniques and new fruit introductions as well.

American Association of Nurserymen, 230 Southern Bldg., Washington, DC 20005.

The American Pomological Society, 103 Tyson Bldg., Pennsylvania State University, University Park, PA 16802.

North American Fruit Explorers, Box 711, St. Louis, MO 63188.

California Rare Fruit Growers, Inc., Fullerton Arboretum, California State University, Fullerton, CA 92634.

New York State Fruit Testing Cooperative Association, Inc., Box 462, Geneva, NY 14456.

The Northern Nut Growers Association, 4518 Holston Mills Rd., Knoxville, TN 37914.

Southern Fruit Council, RR #3, Box 40, Summit, MS 39666.

Horticultural Libraries

One of the most rewarding pursuits for a gardener is to make an exploratory flight from time to time into the classic and rare gardening and horticultural books of the past, in addition to keeping up with the new material being published. A number of libraries in this country have extraordinary horticultural holdings of importance not only to scholars but to advanced gardeners as well. Here are some of the best specialized libraries:

Los Angeles State and County Arboretum Plant Science Library, 301 N. Baldwin Ave., Arcadia, CA 91006

Helen Crocker Russell Library of Horticulture, 9th Ave. at Lincoln Way, San Francisco, CA 94122

Helen K. Fowler Library, Denver Botanic Gardens, 1005 York St., Denver, CO 80206

Smithsonian Institution Libraries, Natural History Bldg., Washington, DC 20560

U.S. National Arboretum Library, Washington, DC 20002

Chicago Horticultural Society Library, Botanic Garden, P.O. Box 400, Glencoe, IL 60022

Massachusetts Horticultural Society Library, 300 Massachusetts Ave., Boston, MA 02115

Arnold Arboretum Library, Harvard University, 22 Divinity Ave., Cambridge, MA 02318

Michigan Horticultural Society, The White House, Belle Isle, Detroit, MI 48207

St. Paul Campus Library, University of Minnesota, St. Paul, MN 55108

Missouri Botanical Garden Library, 2345 Tower Grove Ave., St. Louis, MO 63110

C. Y. Thompson Library, University of Nebraska, Lincoln, NE 68503

Biological Sciences Library, Kendall Hall, University of New Hampshire, Durham, NH 03824

Cook College, Rutgers University, New Brunswick, NJ 08903

New York Botanical Garden Library, Bronx, NY 10458.

Brooklyn Botanic Garden Library, 1000 Washington Ave., Brooklyn, NY 11225

Albert R. Mann Library, Cornell University, Ithaca, NY 14853

The Horticultural Society of New York, 128 W. 58th St., New York, NY 10019

Eleanor Squire Library, The Garden Center of Greater Cleveland, 11030 East Blvd., Cleveland, OH 44106

Ohio Agricultural Research & Development Center Library, Wooster, OH 44691

The Morris Arboretum, University of Pennsylvania, 9414 Meadowbrook Ave., Philadelphia, PA 19118

The Pennsylvania Horticultural Society, 325 Walnut St., Philadelphia, PA 19106.

Hilton M. Briggs Library, South Dakota State University, Brookings, SD 57006

Special Sources of Plant Material

Plant societies are sources of information on dealers in special and rare plant material, but many gardeners spend years looking for certain cultivars half-remembered from childhood days or elusively described in old books but never discovered in modern catalogs. There are a number of plant and seed search sources that serve gardeners for a fee. Here are two of them:

HHH Horticultural, 68 Brooktree Rd., Hightstown, NJ 08520, offers two annual guides to mail-order nurseries: *The Hardy Plant Finder* and *The Tender Plant Finder.*

Plant Search, 1328 Motor Circle, Dallas, TX 75207, is an organization with an enormous, updated collection of catalogs on seed, plant, and bulb sources. They will forward the source addresses and prices to gardeners for a fee.

There are many companies specializing in rare and exotic plants. You may want to write for the catalogs of dealers in special plant material. Here is a listing of a few of these firms. Your local horticultural society may be able to steer you to other sources of specialty plants in your area. Seed sources are listed in the next section of this book.

Endangered Species, 12571 Redhill Ave., Tustin, CA 92680. The rarest plants.

Logee's Greenhouses, 55 North St., Danielson, CT 06239. Rare house plants.

John Brudy's Rare Plant House, Box 1348, Cocoa Beach, FL 32931. Rare tropical plants.

Caladium World, Box 525, Sebring, FL 33870. Caladiums.

Greenworld Products, Box 1423, Winter Haven, FL 32703. Jungle-collected orchids.

Singers' Growing Things, 17806 Plummer St., Northridge, GA 91324. Exotic and unusual plants.

Hawaiian Sunshine Nursery, Box 353, Haleiwa, HI 96712. Rare tropical plants.

Thon's Garden Mums, 4811 Oak St., Crystal Lake, IL 60014. Chrysanthemums.

Shields Horticultural Gardens, Box 92, Westfield, IN 46074. Unusual bulbs.

Cook's Geranium Nursery, 712 N. Grand St., Lyons, KS 67554. Geraniums.

International Growers Exchange, Farmington, MI 48024. Rare bulbs and plants.

Makielski Berry Farm & Nursery, 7130 Platt Rd., Ypsilanti, MI 48197. Raspberries and other berries.

Harry Leuthardt Nurseries, Inc., E. Moriches, Long Island, NY 11940. Dwarf espaliered fruit trees.

Gossler Farms Nursery, 1200 Weaver Rd., Springfield, OR 97477. Magnolias.

Swan Island Dahlias, Box 800, Canby, OR 97103. Dahlias.

Matsu-Momiji Nursery, Box 11414, Philadelphia, PA 19111. Rare Japanese maples and pines.

Putney Nursery, Putney, VT 05346. Wild flowers, herbs, ferns.

Specialty Books Worth Looking At

Hundreds of gardening books are published every year, and only horticultural librarians can keep up with them all. But here are a few old and new books worth noting:

Clarence and Eleanor Birdseye, *Growing Woodland Plants.* New York: Dover Books, 1972. This excellent little book, first published in 1951, continues to flourish.

Hal Bruce, *How to Grow Wildflowers and Wild Shrubs and Trees in Your Own Garden.* New York: Alfred A. Knopf, 1976. An excellent book by a well-known horticultural writer.

Mary Ross Duffield and Warren D. Jones, *Plants for Dry Climates.* Tucson, Ariz.: HP Books, 1982. A useful new book on southwestern plants.

Charles Marden Fitch, *All About Orchids.* Garden City, N.Y.: Doubleday & Co., 1982. One of the best introductory books on orchid growing.

Geri Harrington, *Grow Your Own Chinese Vegetables.* New York: Collier Books, 1978. Tremendously helpful for those of us who love Chinese and Japanese cooking. An unusual section is devoted to oriental water plants such as Chinese lotus, water chestnuts, violet-stemmed taro, and arrowhead, with cultural directions.

Thomas Hay, *Plants for the Connoisseur.* New York: Macmillan, 1938. Descriptions and cultural notes on exotic plants from all over the world by the then-superintendent of London's parks.

Robert Hendrickson, *The Berry Book.* New York: Doubleday & Co., 1981. This book looks at the culture, uses, and propagation of 50 berries in 500 different cultivars. Includes a list of 50 mulches suitable for berries and lists 78 berry dealers. Indispensable for the small fruit grower.

William L. Hunt, *Southern Gardening.* Durham, N.C.: Duke University Press, 1982. An excellent book on regional growing.

Cecile Hulse Matschat, *Mexican Plants for American Gardens.* Boston: Houghton Mifflin Co., 1935. An extraordinary book long out of print but still of use to gardeners in the southwest.

Mildred and Edward Thompson, *Begonias: The Complete Reference Guide.* New York: Times Books, 1982. A very rich begonia book by two experts.

You can use the following pages to make notes on any new techniques you want to try out, plant dealers and nurseries whose catalogs you want to order, special books you want to buy or check out from the library, or groups or institutions you want to contact.

Notes

Blooming Time — 1989

Crocus — late Feb. & March — all finished by mid-March

Hyacinth & Wood Hyacinth — late March

Forsythia — middle March — gone in last few days 4/15

Andromeda — mid. March

Daphne — mid-March

Daffodils — started about 3rd week in March

Grecian Wind Flowers — mid Feb. start, highth of bloom at end of March — still blooming, 4/15/89.

Unique rhododendrons — now in bloom 4/15

Tulips — started early April.

Fruit Trees — April — full bloom now, 4/15

Ornamental apple — coming into bloom 4/15

Rhododendron — Ramapo and Cream Crest & purple by S. end of bridge (may be a Ramapo also), David — just starting. 4/15

Azaleas — red ones by dry creek, Vuyk's Scarlet & Traditions, Hino Crimson 4/15 and purple bushes in front yard.

Early Iris — low, dark purple — 4/15

Violets have been in bloom about 2/3 weeks — still blooming 4/15

Pink phlox by street 4/15

Virginia Roberts Rhody just begining 4/23 — by front door.

Pink Camelia has been in bloom for a month — still has some bloom 4/23

Notes

Notes

From Seed to Harvest

The tiny seeds that spill from the purchased packet represent years—even centuries—of selective plant breeding, and the future harvest from your garden is enclosed within them. There are hundreds of seed companies in North America, but few grow their own seed. Seed is most often grown commercially in other regions of the world—from Guatemala to Taiwan—places that have good climates for seed maturation and low labor costs, for the hand pollination necessary to produce many hybrids is expensive.

Many companies buy seed from the same source, but others own their own growing fields and harvest exclusive plant cultivars developed by their breeders. Often the genetic material in these seeds has been tailored to northern or difficult growing areas. Some seed companies, such as Stokes, list the country of seed origin on the packet. Others, like Harris and Johnny's Selected Seeds, do their own breeding and carefully select cultivars that are suited to the North. Some seedsmen deal in European seeds or the seeds of exotic plants. The range is wide and the catalogs alluring.

Generally, it is better to buy seeds from a mail-order catalog rather than a supermarket or hardware store rack. The mail-order seeds are fresh and often vacuum sealed, where store seed racks may stand in harsh sunlight and heat that rob them of their vigor and reduce the germination rate. Seeds are living entities that must be carefully stored.

Major seed companies are well known to gardeners, and every gardening periodical carries advertisements for their catalogs. Sometimes, however, the advanced gardener wants special seed material that the major houses do not find it profitable to carry, or rare seed that is in very short supply. The L. H. Bailey Hortatorium, Cornell University, Ithaca, NY 14850, has the world's largest collection of current seed catalogs. These are indexed, and for a fee the Hortatorium will send information on the commercial sources of plant seeds. Another organization, Plant Search, 1328 Motor Circle, Dallas, TX 75207, also has an enormous catalog collection on seed, bulb, and plant sources, and will send you source addresses and prices of seed you are searching for, for a fee. Write for information.

Old and unusual vegetable varieties can be exchanged through Kent Whealy's Seed Saver's Exchange, RR #2, Princeton, MO 64673. Mr. Whealy has set up this seed exchange service to preserve the vegetable cultivar gene bank. Plant breeders, seed companies, and everyday gardeners are all linked together through his exchange list. There's a $3 fee. Write for information and application forms.

For information on seed banks, a copy of *Seed Banks Serving People—Proceedings of a Workshop,* can be purchased for $3.50 from:

Meals for Millions, Box 42622, Tucson, AZ 85733.

Specialty Seed Houses

There are numerous sources of unusual and rare seeds, and the list below will direct you to some of them. Companies which specialize in certain areas are so noted; the others offer a more varied selection of seeds.

Alaska Yukon Plant and Seed Co., Box 5499, North Pole, AK 99705. Short-season cultivars.

Tsang & Ma International, Box 294, Belmont, CA 94002. Chinese plant seeds.

Exotica Seed Co., 1742 Laurel Canyon Blvd., Los Angeles, CA 90046. Exotics and tropicals.

J. L. Hudson, Seedsman, Box 1058, Redwood City, CA 94064.

Redwood City Seed Co., Box 361, Redwood City, CA 94064.

Kitazawa Seed Co., 356 W. Taylor St., San Jose, CA 95110. Oriental plant seeds.

Sassafras Farms, Box 1007, Topanga, CA 90290.

Wilton's Organic Potatoes, Box 38, Aspen, CO 81611. Seed potatoes.

Sunrise Enterprises, Box 10058, Elmwood, CT 06110. Oriental plant seeds.

Butterbrooke Farm, 78 Barry Rd., Oxford, CT 06483.

John Brudy Exotics, Box 1348, Cocoa Beach, FL 32931. Exotic plant seed.

Keo Entities, 348 Chelsea Circle, Land O' Lakes, FL 33539. Seeds of rare and exotic plants.

J. A. Demonchaux, 827 N. Kansas Ave., Topeka, KS 66608. French seed imports.

Reuter's Seed Co., 320 N. Carrollton Ave., New Orleans, LA 70119.

Johnny's Selected Seeds, Albion, ME 04910. Seeds for short-season areas.

Pinetree Seed Co., Box 1399, Portland, ME 04104.

Dr. Yoo Farm, Box 290, College Park, MD 20740. Oriental seeds.

Cameron Seeds, 4141 Springhill Rd., Bozeman, MT 59515.

The Fragrant Path, Box 328, Ft. Calhoun, NE 68023. Seeds of fragrant plants, shrubs, trees.

Thompson & Morgan, Box 100, Farmingdale, NJ 07727. Extraordinarily large number of varieties.

Grace's Garden, Autumn La., Hackettstown, NJ 07840. Novelty plant seed.

Plants of the Southwest, 1570 Pacheco St., Santa Fe, NM 87501.

Japonica Nursery, Box 236, Larchmont, NY 10538. Seeds of Japanese cultivars.

Epicure Seeds, Ltd., Box 23568, Rochester, NY 14692. Imported European seeds.

The Urban Farmer, 22000 Halburton Rd., Beachwood, OH 44122. Domestic and imported seeds of dwarf plants for space-restricted gardeners.

Taroka Co., Box 5, Warren, OH 44482. Oriental plant seeds.

Nichols Garden Nursery, 1190 N. Pacific Hwy., Albany, OR 97321. Large selection of rare vegetable and herb seeds.

Horticultural Enterprises, Box 34082, Dallas, TX 75234. Mexican plant seeds and lots of chili peppers.

Willhite Melon Seed Farms, Box 85, Weatherford, TX 76086. Melon seeds.

Vermont Bean Seed Co., Garden La., Bomoseen, VT 05732. Very large collection of corn, pea, and bean seeds.

Elysian Hills, Dummerston, VT 05301. Gilfeather turnips.

Le Jardin du Gourmet, West Danville, VT 05873. French seed imports.

McLaughlin Seeds, Box 550, Mead, WA 99021. Oriental plant seeds.

Abundant Life Seed Foundation, Box 722, Port Townsend, WA 98368.

William Dam Seeds, Hwy. 8, West Flamboro, ON L0R 0K0, Canada.

There are several good books out on starting seeds, but one stands head and shoulders above the others. Ann Reilly, *Park's Success with Seeds* (Greenwood, S.C.: Geo. W. Park Co., 1978) is a tremendously useful tool for beginning and expert gardeners alike. Lavishly illustrated, the encyclopedic chapter 5 contains photographs of the mature plant and the seedling and gives its uses, habit, germination tips, and cultural advice all on a concise page. The only fault is the lack of information on saving your own seed, and this lack is filled by Marc Rogers, *Growing and Saving Vegetable Seeds* (Charlotte, Vt.: Garden Way Publishing Co., 1978).

Seed Treatments

Not all seeds can be sown directly in the garden or flats as they come from the packet—some demand special treatment, such as scarification, a period of total darkness or light exposure, or soaking before they will germinate. The seeds of many woody or tropical plants are shipped fresh in damp sphagnum moss right after they are havested. These seeds must be planted *at once,* and it is the kiss of death to let them dry out. Other seeds, such as delphinium, geranium, potentilla, certain lilies, and others have short lives and will not keep long in any kind of storage.

Scarification means scratching or nicking the very hard coats of such seeds as morning glories, beets, spinach, petunias, palm trees, and others. Many are mechanically scarified by the seedsman before they are shipped, but some are not. (Sometimes the seed package will note whether or not the seeds have been scarified. If it does not carry such a notice, you can play it safe and scarify the seeds yourself.) Some seeds have thick, oily coats which retard germination. Asparagus, lupin, moonflower vine, morning glory, okra, and sweet pea seeds can be rolled gently between two wood blocks covered with sandpaper until the water-resistant coat is worn on ridges and corners. Then the seeds should be scrubbed with your hands in two cups of warm, soapy (no detergent!) water. Let the seeds soak overnight in the water, then blot on a paper towel and plant them immediately the next day.

Nasturtium, parsley, beet, and parsnip seeds germinate one to two weeks faster if soaked overnight in warm, soapy water. They do not need to be sandpapered. Water for soaking seeds should be no hotter than 190°F, or the embryonic plant may be injured or even killed. The seeds should never dry out after soaking.

Canna seeds (called Indian shot because of their shape and hardness) actually must be filed or slightly clipped with nail clippers to dent the coat, then soaked in warm, soapy water before they will give a good germination rate.

Seeds should be handled by the home gardener in relation to size as well as other special treatments demanded by the kind of plant. Large seeds, such as zinnia, corn, peas, beans, and sunflowers, have large reservoirs of food in their tissues and sprout quickly and vigorously. Small seeds are enormously variable in their germination times; cabbage sprouts in four days while parsley can take three weeks to venture forth. Direct-seeded small seeds have a higher germination rate when the seed bed is well watered and raked fine, for close contact with the soil particles is crucial in keeping the seeds damp enough to sprout. Fine seeds should be started indoors and grown to decent size before they are set out in the garden. Direct-seeding fine seed is very risky, for these mites are easy to bury, or may wash away in the rain or dry out and die before they sprout. It takes a very good gardener with a skillful hand to direct-seed fine seed.

One of the best garden gadgets to come down the pike in a long while is the hand-held seed spacer, a small plastic container with an adjustable gate to sort different sizes of seeds. These gadgets space out seeds very evenly when tapped lightly. Damp seeds tend to stick in them, however.

Seed Planting Tips

Slow-sprouting seeds, such as parsley, beets, and onions, do very well if the newly seeded bed is covered with damp burlap. Spray the burlap with water several times each day, and check under it often. In the warm, damp environment seeds germinate rapidly. When the

---

The Best Way to Plant Seeds

1. A proper seedbed has soil particles the size of coffee grounds. Till or spade the seedbed area, water it heavily, and *let the soil settle.* When the surface soil is dry enough to work, rake and rake and rake until the seedbed is smooth and level.
2. Key the furrow sizes to the seed sizes. Large seeds get furrows 1 to 2 inches deep, made with a corner of the hoe. Small seeds benefit from a shallow furrow about ½ inch deep. It is simple to make such a furrow by lightly pressing the edge of a board into the prepared soil. If you are doing wide row planting, press down a wide board.
3. Space the seeds far enough apart to save yourself the labor of thinning.
4. For highest germination rates, cover small seeds with sand or sieved compost instead of soil. The sprouting time and germination rate is much better.
5. Mist the planted seedbed two or three times a day until the sprouts emerge, and twice a day for another week after they're up.

Trellised melons need support. This one is tied up in a simple raffia sling while still small.

sprouts are up, remove the burlap gradually.

Presprouting is a simple technique that is especially useful with slow starters like beets, parsley, delphinium, and larkspur. Place a handful or so of milled dry sphagnum moss (do not use peat moss, which lacks the disease-inhibiting qualities of sphagnum) on an old towel and roll up the towel. Then moisten the towel and twist it to force moisture into the moss. Let the towel stand an hour, then twist and wring it again. The moisture the moss has absorbed is all that is needed to get the seeds going.

Write the seed variety on a small plastic bag with a marking pen, then put in a cup of moist moss and a pinch of seeds. Shake until moss and seeds are well mixed, then twist the bag closed. Put the bag on the warm spot on top of the refrigerator and let nature take its course. When about half the seeds have put out rootlets (between 5 and 20 days, depending on the cultivar), plant in the garden. Be sure the furrow is prepared in advance and damp.

Work very quickly, for exposure to wind or sun can kill the sprouts. Cover the sprouts in the furrow with sieved compost or sand, as for fine seeds. Mist the sprouts twice a day until they emerge from the soil.

Indoor Seed-Starting in Flats

One of the best ways to start plants inside is in flats. Unfortunately, it is easy to get cultivars mixed up in flats unless you post tiny markers and make sure to shift them with the seedlings when you set them out to harden off in the cold frame and then shift them once more to the garden. Flat diagrams provide a paper record of what's planted where and allow you to make detailed notes in your record book that will be useful for years. To use the flat diagrams on the following pages, number your flats and simply indicate on the diagram which seeds are planted where. Detailed information should go on the pages following the flat diagrams, From Seed to Harvest.

Flat Diagrams   Planting Boxes

Flat #1

Flat #2

Flat #3

Flat #4

Flat Diagrams

From Seed to Harvest

Species & Cultivar	Company	Country of Origin	Cost	Amount in Packet	Date Started	Germi-nation Rate	Special Cultural Notes

Transplanted	Hardened Off or Cold Frame	Set in Garden	Water, Fertilizer, Progress Notes	Date Mature Fruit	Amount Harvested	Comments

From Seed to Harvest

Species & Cultivar	Company	Country of Origin	Cost	Amount in Packet	Date Started	Germination Rate	Special Cultural Notes

Transplanted	Hardened Off or Cold Frame	Set in Garden	Water, Fertilizer, Progress Notes	Date Mature Fruit	Amount Harvested	Comments

From Seed to Harvest

Species & Cultivar	Company	Country of Origin	Cost	Amount in Packet	Date Started	Germi- nation Rate	Special Cultural Notes

Transplanted	Hardened Off or Cold Frame	Set in Garden	Water, Fertilizer, Progress Notes	Date Mature Fruit	Amount Harvested	Comments

Weather and Phenology

This section is the heart of your gardening records. The accumulated notations of precipitation, frosts, cloud formations, drought, prevailing winds, the path of sunlight over the garden area, the maximum and minimum temperatures, the date buds on certain indicator plants emerge, the date of flowering, the return and departure of migrating birds, the amount of deadwood on trees and shrubs after the winter—all these can help you identify microclimates best for growing on your property, and tell you when to plant in the spring. For example, zone maps are constructed on information and data taken from weather instruments in standard shelters built at uniform heights—150 centimeters above ground level. This height is deliberately calculated to exclude ground level influences on the meteorological instruments, and the collated data gives us extremely useful information on the macroclimate. However, those very ground level influences that were excluded from the data are extremely important to growth and plant development.

In a nine-year study in Burlington, Vermont, conducted by the late Dr. Richard J. Hopp, it was found that the average date of the last occurrence of 0°C at 7.5 centimeters above the ground—that's about 3 inches above the ground—was *16 days later* than at the standard 150-centimeter height of the instrument shelter. In the fall, the first date for 0°C near the ground was *14 days earlier* than the shelter date. The unappealing conclusion is that the freeze-free season was 30 days shorter near the ground than at the 150-centimeter height.

If you want to know the true length of your growing season precisely at your garden site, you will have to keep temperature and observation records from weather instruments set near the ground. *There is no other source for this information.* Zone maps are simply rough guides to the macroclimate, and to fine-tune climatological data for your immediate surroundings, record-keeping is indispensable.

The growth and development of plants is not tied to the number of days listed on the back of the seed packet, but to the actual growing and weather conditions in their immediate surroundings, particularly air and soil temperatures. Solar thermal units and growing degree-days are both relatively new measurements designed to correlate with plant growth. An excellent introduction to observing, noting, and interpreting weather measurements and signs is James J. Rahn, *Making the Weather Work for You* (Charlotte, Vt.: Garden Way Publishing Co., 1979).

Microclimates

Microclimates are very small, local environmental conditions that are affected (and changed) by walls, buildings, windbreaks, plants and trees, and the slope and shape of the land. Although the USDA Zone Map may show that you live in a frigid Zone 3, a sheltered south slope protected on the north by walls and buildings, the force of the westerly wind broken by a shelterbelt or windbreak, can be a small oasis of Zone 5 where plants and shrubs will grow that haven't a chance 50 feet outside the microclimate. Every property has such sheltered, warm spots, and keen observation can help you identify them.

Conversely, every property has adverse microclimates—damp, low-lying sinks or exposed north slopes where frost and wind are constant enemies. The observant gardener will identify these, too. Microclimates can be made or changed by judicious placement of buildings, hedges, fencing, and shelter walls. The movement of cold air is much like water; cold air tends to drain downward into frost pockets. If you have several thermometers, you can chart the different temperature levels at different locations on your property. Armed with the resulting data, you can select the ideal garden sites.

Phenology

Phenology is the study of the time of recurrence of biological events, the observation of life-cycle phases, and the activities of animals and plants through the year. Records of key phenological indicators allow you to construct a phenological calendar to guide your gardening based on natural events and times of plant growth within your immediate locale. The observation of certain key plants at phenological observation stations across the country has been extremely useful to farmers and agricultural agents in predicting the ripening dates of fruit, grains, and berries, and in indicating safe, frost-free times to plant.

We are all aware of phenological changes, for the change of seasons is part of our own biological rhythms. Every spring a "green wave" sweeps northward at a rate of about 100 miles a day, and plant life begins to surge from the ground once again. In autumn the "brown wave" sinks southward, leaving a dull, monochromatic, and quiescent landscape behind it. These major changes are easy to note, but more detailed observations of plant changes can be of inestimable use to gardeners.

Phenological observations have been used for thousands of years in crop growing. Early New England farmers planted corn by Indian custom, keyed to phenological observations of foliage development—safe to plant corn when elm leaves were the size of a squirrel's ear or oak leaves matched the size of a mouse's ear. Persian lilacs have been used as phenological indicators in this country

for several decades, and the data has been keyed to small grain cropping as well as garden planting times. The Persian lilac is a good phenological indicator plant because it is hardy, resistant to drought and heat, easy to propagate vegetatively, and quite resistant to insects and diseases, and because it has conspicuous phenological phases. Dr. Richard J. Hopp of the University of Vermont did considerable work with lilacs and phenological phases, and the agricultural experiment bulletins listed at the end of this section will be of use in establishing your own phenological lilac observation garden.

Generally, observers look for four basic phenological phases in the lilac:

1. First leaf.
2. First flowers.
3. Full bloom.
4. End of bloom.

Dr. Hopp suggested that home gardeners could plant cool-season crops, such as peas, beets, and lettuce, before or during the first-leaf stage, and that by the time the indicator lilacs were in full bloom, warm-season crops, such as corn, beans, and cucumbers, could be sown without much to fear from frost damage.

However, one-time observations are not very reliable; a longer term collection of data obviously gives you a better data base from which to draw your conclusions. It is also useful to farmers and gardeners to work out relationships between insect outbreaks and plant indicators. The European corn borer emergence has been keyed to the blooming date of *Viburnum dentatum*. Forsythia blossoming on Long Island is a reliable indicator of the arrival of adult cabbage maggots, though farther north, in sections of Massachusetts, the average date of observed cabbage maggot eggs is keyed to the full pink stage of McIntosh apple blossom buds.

It may take the observant gardener a few years to work out useful relationships between weather, phenological signs, insect phases, planting times, and plant growth, so that records are indispensable. Sometimes your plant indicators will leaf early through unusually warm spring weather, or late because of cold, stormy days. If your records show an unseasonably warm May, for example, and show that your indicator lilac has bloomed a week early in comparison with the dates of the last few years, then temper the urge to plant with your statistical knowledge that this is a forward year, and wait a week.

The home gardener is in a better position to observe,

record, and use phenological data that relates to his or her own immediate surroundings than any scientific body collecting more general data. A good observer and record keeper can tailor garden and cropland culture to the natural signs. Look for the first leaves, the first flowers, full bloom. Notice wildflowers, insect appearances; be aware of bird migrations and courting behavior. Whatever you see, write down, for good records are the basis of good gardening. The record will have use far beyond the call of your garden and grounds. It becomes a diary of the natural world around you.

Books and Bulletins on Phenology. The following sources contain helpful phenological information:

Helmut Lieth, ed., *Phenology and Seasonality Modeling.* New York, Heidelberg, Berlin: Springer-Verlag, 1974. Scholarly, but with an invaluable phenology bibliography.

R. J. Hopp, "Charting the Progress of Spring," *Weekly Weather Crop Bulletin.* Apr. 17, 1971, p. 12.

_____, "Phenology: An Aid to Agricultural Technology," Vermont Agricultural Experiment Station Bulletin 684, 1978.

R. J. Hopp et al., *Plant Phenology in Eastern and Central North America.* I. "Development of Networks and Preliminary Results," Vt. Agr. Exp. Sta. Bull. 677, 1973. II. "Phenological Observations on Lilac 'Red Rothomagensis'," Vt. Agr. Exp. Sta. Bull. 678, 1973.

R. J. Hopp et al., "Instructions for Phenological Observations: Persian Lilac," Vt. Agr. Exp. Sta., Pamphlet 36, 1969.

The Vermont Agricultural Experiment Station publications may be ordered from:

Vermont Publications, The Extension Service, Agricultural Experiment Station, University of Vermont, Burlington, VT 05401.

J. M. Caprio et al., "Instructions for Phenological Observations of Purple Common Lilacs and Red Berry Honeysuckle," Montana Agr. Exp. Sta. Circ. 250. Order this publication from:

Publications, Agricultural Experiment Station, Bozeman, MT 59715.

Aids in Observing Weather

Most seed suppliers and garden supply houses offer maximum/minimum thermometers, rain gauges, and

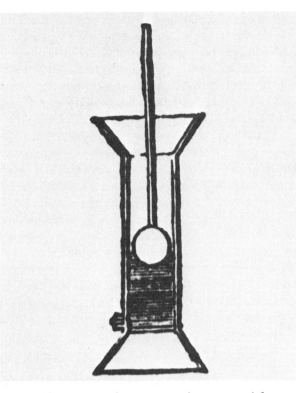

An early nineteenth-century rain gauge with a calibrated stem attached to a cork float.

simple wind speed gauges. The weather instrument suppliers listed in James Rahn's *Making the Weather Work for You* are almost all sources of highly sophisticated, very expensive professional meteorological equipment, far beyond the needs or purses of most home gardeners. The exception is Weatherwise Books and Instruments, 68 Browning Ave., Nashua, NH 03062, which offers an excellent list of books on weather of great use to the gardener, and dozens of basic, high-quality instruments at a moderate cost.

Gardeners who wish to get serious about weather recording should request the catalog of Science Associates, Box 230-8, Princeton, NJ 08540. Science Associates also stocks an excellent wall Cloud Chart.

Weatherwise is a fascinating bimonthly weather publication of interest to any sky-watcher. Write to:

Weatherwise, Heldref Publications, 4000 Albemarle St. NW, Washington, DC 20016.

A small weather prediction instrument using a series of cards with cloud photographs, seasonal data, and wind settings is available for about $25 from Weatherwise Books and Instruments (listed above). It is called Pocket

1831. June	Thermometer.			Baro-meter.	Rain and Hail.	Wind.	General character of the day's weather.	Trees in Leaf, or defo-liated. Fungi appear, &c.	Plants in Flower or Fruit.	Birds and Insects ap-pear or dis-appear.	Observ-ations as to Fish and other Ani-mals.	Miscellane-ous. Bodily Pains, pre-vailing Dis-eases, &c.
	M.	N.	E.									
21	50	71	60	28·90	0·	S. S.W.	Fair.	Marchántia polymórpha in perfec-tion.	Lílium cán-didum in full blow.	Sphínx Elpènor appears.	Spawn of the Carp hatched in breeding pond.	Dull and sleepy.
22	52	69	58	28·8	0·02	S.W.	Showers.					
23	51	65	59	28·8	0·00	S.	Cloudy.		Nùphar ádve-na in flower.			
24	58	70	58	28·7	0·01	S.W.	Windy.			———	Ditto Bream.	Well and in high spirits.

A sample of an early weather and phenological journal. Notice the interesting section for noting down one's mood and bodily sensa-tions. Such observations, jotted down over a period of time, could make the gardener's body a meteorological forecasting instrument.

Weather Trend Single Station Analysis Instrument and was developed by Air Force meteorologists.

Several books about weather observation are worth mentioning:

Tim Campbell, *The Do-It-Yourself Weather Book.* Birmingham, Ala.: Oxmoor House, 1979. Lists dozens of sources of weather information.

Rudolf Geiger, *The Climate Near the Ground.* Cambridge, Mass.: Harvard University Press, 1965. Scholarly but important.

Chang Jen-Hu, *Climate and Agriculture.* Chicago: Aldine Publishing Co., 1968.

David Ludlum, *The Country Journal New England Weather Book.* Boston: Houghton Mifflin Co., 1976. Both entertaining and practical as well as lavishly illustrated.

Calvin Simonds, *The Weather-Wise Gardener: A Guide to Understanding, Predicting, and Working with the Weather.* Emmaus, Pa.: Rodale Press, 1983. Lucidly written treatise on weather from a gardener's point of view. Excellent explanations of how weather works, how to predict the weather in one's own backyard, and how to protect both gardener and garden from extreme conditions.

The following pages are for you to record, each day, weather conditions and phenological observations, along with the progress of your garden. At the end of the year, you will have an immensely useful picture of the micro-climates on your property and the basis of an individual gardening guide based on the climatic conditions right in your garden rather than on the generalized information derived from hardiness zones. Use these pages in whatever way will be most useful to you.

For example, if your primary interest is in ascertaining your microclimates and becoming familiar with local weather patterns, you will want to record daily maximum and minimum temperatures at several locations on your property, along with wind direction and velocity, frost and precipitation, and predominating types of clouds.

If you are more concerned about phenology, pay particular attention to indicators such as the leafing out, budding, and blooming of trees and shrubs, wildflowers, and other native plants on and around your property, arrival and departure of insects (both beneficials and pests) and birds, and growth of other local weeds and wildlife.

Also be sure to make notes on the overall progress of your garden plants, so that you will be able later on to compare their growth and development with your observations of climate, weather, and phenology in your backyard.

Date _____

Weather Observations:

Phenological Observations:

Garden/Plant Notes:

Date _____

Weather Observations:

Phenological Observations:

Garden/Plant Notes:

Date _____

Weather Observations:

Phenological Observations:

Garden/Plant Notes:

Date _____

Weather Observations:

Phenological Observations:

Garden/Plant Notes:

Date _____

Weather Observations:

Phenological Observations:

Garden/Plant Notes:

Date _____

Weather Observations:

Phenological Observations:

Garden/Plant Notes:

Date _____

Weather Observations:

Phenological Observations:

Garden/Plant Notes:

Date _____

Weather Observations:

Phenological Observations:

Garden/Plant Notes:

Date _____

Weather Observations:

Phenological Observations:

Garden/Plant Notes:

Date _____

Weather Observations:

Phenological Observations:

Garden/Plant Notes:

Date _____

Weather Observations:

Phenological Observations:

Garden/Plant Notes:

Date _____

Weather Observations:

Phenological Observations:

Garden/Plant Notes:

Date _____

Weather Observations:

Phenological Observations:

Garden/Plant Notes:

Date _____

Weather Observations:

Phenological Observations:

Garden/Plant Notes:

Date _____

Weather Observations:

Phenological Observations:

Garden/Plant Notes:

Date _____

Weather Observations:

Phenological Observations:

Garden/Plant Notes:

Date _____

Weather Observations:

Phenological Observations:

Garden/Plant Notes:

Date _____

Weather Observations:

Phenological Observations:

Garden/Plant Notes:

Date _____

Weather Observations:

Phenological Observations:

Garden/Plant Notes:

Date _____

Weather Observations:

Phenological Observations:

Garden/Plant Notes:

Date _____

Weather Observations:

Phenological Observations:

Garden/Plant Notes:

Date _____

Weather Observations:

Phenological Observations:

Garden/Plant Notes:

Date _____

Weather Observations:

Phenological Observations:

Garden/Plant Notes:

Date _____

Weather Observations:

Phenological Observations:

Garden/Plant Notes:

Date _____

Weather Observations:

Phenological Observations:

Garden/Plant Notes:

Date _____

Weather Observations:

Phenological Observations:

Garden/Plant Notes:

Date _____

Weather Observations:

Phenological Observations:

Garden/Plant Notes:

Date _____

Weather Observations:

Phenological Observations:

Garden/Plant Notes:

Date _____

Weather Observations:

Phenological Observations:

Garden/Plant Notes:

Date _____

Weather Observations:

Phenological Observations:

Garden/Plant Notes:

Date _____

Weather Observations:

Phenological Observations:

Garden/Plant Notes:

Date _____

Weather Observations:

Phenological Observations:

Garden/Plant Notes:

Date _____

Weather Observations:

Phenological Observations:

Garden/Plant Notes:

Date _____

Weather Observations:

Phenological Observations:

Garden/Plant Notes:

Date _____

Weather Observations:

Phenological Observations:

Garden/Plant Notes:

Date _____

Weather Observations:

Phenological Observations:

Garden/Plant Notes:

Date _____

Weather Observations:

Phenological Observations:

Garden/Plant Notes:

Date _____

Weather Observations:

Phenological Observations:

Garden/Plant Notes:

Date _____

Weather Observations:

Phenological Observations:

Garden/Plant Notes:

Date _____

Weather Observations:

Phenological Observations:

Garden/Plant Notes:

Date _____

Weather Observations:

Phenological Observations:

Garden/Plant Notes:

Date _____

Weather Observations:

Phenological Observations:

Garden/Plant Notes:

Date _____

Weather Observations:

Phenological Observations:

Garden/Plant Notes:

Date _____

Weather Observations:

Phenological Observations:

Garden/Plant Notes:

Date _____

Weather Observations:

Phenological Observations:

Garden/Plant Notes:

Date _____

Weather Observations:

Phenological Observations:

Garden/Plant Notes:

Date _____

Weather Observations:

Phenological Observations:

Garden/Plant Notes:

Date _____

Weather Observations:

Phenological Observations:

Garden/Plant Notes:

Date _____

Weather Observations:

Phenological Observations:

Garden/Plant Notes:

Date _____

Weather Observations:

Phenological Observations:

Garden/Plant Notes:

Date _____

Weather Observations:

Phenological Observations:

Garden/Plant Notes:

Date _____

Weather Observations:

Phenological Observations:

Garden/Plant Notes:

Date _____

Weather Observations:

Phenological Observations:

Garden/Plant Notes:

Date _____

Weather Observations:

Phenological Observations:

Garden/Plant Notes:

Date _____

Weather Observations:

Phenological Observations:

Garden/Plant Notes:

Date _____

Weather Observations:

Phenological Observations:

Garden/Plant Notes:

Date _____

Weather Observations:

Phenological Observations:

Garden/Plant Notes:

Date _____

Weather Observations:

Phenological Observations:

Garden/Plant Notes:

Date _____

Weather Observations:

Phenological Observations:

Garden/Plant Notes:

Date _____

Weather Observations:

Phenological Observations:

Garden/Plant Notes:

Date _____

Weather Observations:

Phenological Observations:

Garden/Plant Notes:

Date _____

Weather Observations:

Phenological Observations:

Garden/Plant Notes:

Date _____

Weather Observations:

Phenological Observations:

Garden/Plant Notes:

Date _____

Weather Observations:

Phenological Observations:

Garden/Plant Notes:

Date _____

Weather Observations:

Phenological Observations:

Garden/Plant Notes:

Date _____

Weather Observations:

Phenological Observations:

Garden/Plant Notes:

Date _____

Weather Observations:

Phenological Observations:

Garden/Plant Notes:

Date _____

Weather Observations:

Phenological Observations:

Garden/Plant Notes:

Date _____

Weather Observations:

Phenological Observations:

Garden/Plant Notes:

Date _____

Weather Observations:

Phenological Observations:

Garden/Plant Notes:

Date _____

Weather Observations:

Phenological Observations:

Garden/Plant Notes:

Date _____

Weather Observations:

Phenological Observations:

Garden/Plant Notes:

Date _____

Weather Observations:

Phenological Observations:

Garden/Plant Notes:

Date _____

Weather Observations:

Phenological Observations:

Garden/Plant Notes:

Date _____

Weather Observations:

Phenological Observations:

Garden/Plant Notes:

Date _____

Weather Observations:

Phenological Observations:

Garden/Plant Notes:

Date _____

Weather Observations:

Phenological Observations:

Garden/Plant Notes:

Date _____

Weather Observations:

Phenological Observations:

Garden/Plant Notes:

Date _____

Weather Observations:

Phenological Observations:

Garden/Plant Notes:

Date _____

Weather Observations:

Phenological Observations:

Garden/Plant Notes:

Date _____

Weather Observations:

Phenological Observations:

Garden/Plant Notes:

Date _____

Weather Observations:

Phenological Observations:

Garden/Plant Notes:

Date _____

Weather Observations:

Phenological Observations:

Garden/Plant Notes:

Date _____

Weather Observations:

Phenological Observations:

Garden/Plant Notes:

Date _____

Weather Observations:

Phenological Observations:

Garden/Plant Notes:

Date _____

Weather Observations:

Phenological Observations:

Garden/Plant Notes:

Date _____

Weather Observations:

Phenological Observations:

Garden/Plant Notes:

Date _____

Weather Observations:

Phenological Observations:

Garden/Plant Notes:

Date _____

Weather Observations:

Phenological Observations:

Garden/Plant Notes:

Date _____

Weather Observations:

Phenological Observations:

Garden/Plant Notes:

Date _____

Weather Observations:

Phenological Observations:

Garden/Plant Notes:

Date _____

Weather Observations:

Phenological Observations:

Garden/Plant Notes:

Date _____

Weather Observations:

Phenological Observations:

Garden/Plant Notes:

Date _____

Weather Observations:

Phenological Observations:

Garden/Plant Notes:

Date _____

Weather Observations:

Phenological Observations:

Garden/Plant Notes:

Date _____

Weather Observations:

Phenological Observations:

Garden/Plant Notes:

Date _____

Weather Observations:

Phenological Observations:

Garden/Plant Notes:

Date _____

Weather Observations:

Phenological Observations:

Garden/Plant Notes:

Date _____

Weather Observations:

Phenological Observations:

Garden/Plant Notes:

Date _____

Weather Observations:

Phenological Observations:

Garden/Plant Notes:

Date _____

Weather Observations:

Phenological Observations:

Garden/Plant Notes:

Date _____

Weather Observations:

Phenological Observations:

Garden/Plant Notes:

Date _____

Weather Observations:

Phenological Observations:

Garden/Plant Notes:

Date _____

Weather Observations:

Phenological Observations:

Garden/Plant Notes:

Date _____

Weather Observations:

Phenological Observations:

Garden/Plant Notes:

Date _____

Weather Observations:

Phenological Observations:

Garden/Plant Notes:

Date _____

Weather Observations:

Phenological Observations:

Garden/Plant Notes:

Date _____

Weather Observations:

Phenological Observations:

Garden/Plant Notes:

Date _____

Weather Observations:

Phenological Observations:

Garden/Plant Notes:

Date _____

Weather Observations:

Phenological Observations:

Garden/Plant Notes:

Date _____

Weather Observations:

Phenological Observations:

Garden/Plant Notes:

Date _____

Weather Observations:

Phenological Observations:

Garden/Plant Notes:

Date _____

Weather Observations:

Phenological Observations:

Garden/Plant Notes:

Date _____

Weather Observations:

Phenological Observations:

Garden/Plant Notes:

Date _____

Weather Observations:

Phenological Observations:

Garden/Plant Notes:

Date _____

Weather Observations:

Phenological Observations:

Garden/Plant Notes:

Date _____

Weather Observations:

Phenological Observations:

Garden/Plant Notes:

Date _____

Weather Observations:

Phenological Observations:

Garden/Plant Notes:

Date _____

Weather Observations:

Phenological Observations:

Garden/Plant Notes:

Date _____

Weather Observations:

Phenological Observations:

Garden/Plant Notes:

Date _____

Weather Observations:

Phenological Observations:

Garden/Plant Notes:

Date _____

Weather Observations:

Phenological Observations:

Garden/Plant Notes:

Date _____

Weather Observations:

Phenological Observations:

Garden/Plant Notes:

Date _____

Weather Observations:

Phenological Observations:

Garden/Plant Notes:

Date _____

Weather Observations:

Phenological Observations:

Garden/Plant Notes:

Date _____

Weather Observations:

Phenological Observations:

Garden/Plant Notes:

Date _____

Weather Observations:

Phenological Observations:

Garden/Plant Notes:

Date _____

Weather Observations:

Phenological Observations:

Garden/Plant Notes:

Date _____

Weather Observations:

Phenological Observations:

Garden/Plant Notes:

Date _____

Weather Observations:

Phenological Observations:

Garden/Plant Notes:

Date _____

Weather Observations:

Phenological Observations:

Garden/Plant Notes:

Date _____

Weather Observations:

Phenological Observations:

Garden/Plant Notes:

Date _____

Weather Observations:

Phenological Observations:

Garden/Plant Notes:

Date _____

Weather Observations:

Phenological Observations:

Garden/Plant Notes:

Date _____

Weather Observations:

Phenological Observations:

Garden/Plant Notes:

Date _____

Weather Observations:

Phenological Observations:

Garden/Plant Notes:

Date _____

Weather Observations:

Phenological Observations:

Garden/Plant Notes:

Date _____

Weather Observations:

Phenological Observations:

Garden/Plant Notes:

Date _____

Weather Observations:

Phenological Observations:

Garden/Plant Notes:

Date _____

Weather Observations:

Phenological Observations:

Garden/Plant Notes:

Date _____

Weather Observations:

Phenological Observations:

Garden/Plant Notes:

Date _____

Weather Observations:

Phenological Observations:

Garden/Plant Notes:

Date _____

Weather Observations:

Phenological Observations:

Garden/Plant Notes:

Date _____

Weather Observations:

Phenological Observations:

Garden/Plant Notes:

Date _____

Weather Observations:

Phenological Observations:

Garden/Plant Notes:

Date _____

Weather Observations:

Phenological Observations:

Garden/Plant Notes:

Date _____

Weather Observations:

Phenological Observations:

Garden/Plant Notes:

Date _____

Weather Observations:

Phenological Observations:

Garden/Plant Notes:

Date _____

Weather Observations:

Phenological Observations:

Garden/Plant Notes:

Date _____

Weather Observations:

Phenological Observations:

Garden/Plant Notes:

Date _____

Weather Observations:

Phenological Observations:

Garden/Plant Notes:

Date _____

Weather Observations:

Phenological Observations:

Garden/Plant Notes:

Date _____

Weather Observations:

Phenological Observations:

Garden/Plant Notes:

Date _____

Weather Observations:

Phenological Observations:

Garden/Plant Notes:

Date _____

Weather Observations:

Phenological Observations:

Garden/Plant Notes:

Date _____

Weather Observations:

Phenological Observations:

Garden/Plant Notes:

Date _____

Weather Observations:

Phenological Observations:

Garden/Plant Notes:

Date _____

Weather Observations:

Phenological Observations:

Garden/Plant Notes:

Date _____

Weather Observations:

Phenological Observations:

Garden/Plant Notes:

Date _____

Weather Observations:

Phenological Observations:

Garden/Plant Notes:

Date _____

Weather Observations:

Phenological Observations:

Garden/Plant Notes:

Date _____

Weather Observations:

Phenological Observations:

Garden/Plant Notes:

Date _____

Weather Observations:

Phenological Observations:

Garden/Plant Notes:

Date _____

Weather Observations:

Phenological Observations:

Garden/Plant Notes:

Date _____

Weather Observations:

Phenological Observations:

Garden/Plant Notes:

Date _____

Weather Observations:

Phenological Observations:

Garden/Plant Notes:

Date _____

Weather Observations:

Phenological Observations:

Garden/Plant Notes:

Date _____

Weather Observations:

Phenological Observations:

Garden/Plant Notes:

Date _____

Weather Observations:

Phenological Observations:

Garden/Plant Notes:

Date _____

Weather Observations:

Phenological Observations:

Garden/Plant Notes:

Date _____

Weather Observations:

Phenological Observations:

Garden/Plant Notes:

Date _____

Weather Observations:

Phenological Observations:

Garden/Plant Notes:

Date _____

Weather Observations:

Phenological Observations:

Garden/Plant Notes:

Date _____

Weather Observations:

Phenological Observations:

Garden/Plant Notes:

Date _____

Weather Observations:

Phenological Observations:

Garden/Plant Notes:

Date _____

Weather Observations:

Phenological Observations:

Garden/Plant Notes:

Date _____

Weather Observations:

Phenological Observations:

Garden/Plant Notes:

Date _____

Weather Observations:

Phenological Observations:

Garden/Plant Notes:

Date _____

Weather Observations:

Phenological Observations:

Garden/Plant Notes:

Date _____

Weather Observations:

Phenological Observations:

Garden/Plant Notes:

Date _____

Weather Observations:

Phenological Observations:

Garden/Plant Notes:

Date _____

Weather Observations:

Phenological Observations:

Garden/Plant Notes:

Date _____

Weather Observations:

Phenological Observations:

Garden/Plant Notes:

Date _____

Weather Observations:

Phenological Observations:

Garden/Plant Notes:

Date _____

Weather Observations:

Phenological Observations:

Garden/Plant Notes:

Date _____

Weather Observations:

Phenological Observations:

Garden/Plant Notes:

Date _____

Weather Observations:

Phenological Observations:

Garden/Plant Notes:

Date _____

Weather Observations:

Phenological Observations:

Garden/Plant Notes:

Date _____

Weather Observations:

Phenological Observations:

Garden/Plant Notes:

Date _____

Weather Observations:

Phenological Observations:

Garden/Plant Notes:

Date _____

Weather Observations:

Phenological Observations:

Garden/Plant Notes:

Date _____

Weather Observations:

Phenological Observations:

Garden/Plant Notes:

Date _____

Weather Observations:

Phenological Observations:

Garden/Plant Notes:

Date _____

Weather Observations:

Phenological Observations:

Garden/Plant Notes:

Date _____

Weather Observations:

Phenological Observations:

Garden/Plant Notes:

Date _____

Weather Observations:

Phenological Observations:

Garden/Plant Notes:

Date _____

Weather Observations:

Phenological Observations:

Garden/Plant Notes:

Date _____

Weather Observations:

Phenological Observations:

Garden/Plant Notes:

Date _____

Weather Observations:

Phenological Observations:

Garden/Plant Notes:

Date _____

Weather Observations:

Phenological Observations:

Garden/Plant Notes:

Date _____

Weather Observations:

Phenological Observations:

Garden/Plant Notes:

Date _____

Weather Observations:

Phenological Observations:

Garden/Plant Notes:

Date _____

Weather Observations:

Phenological Observations:

Garden/Plant Notes:

Date _____

Weather Observations:

Phenological Observations:

Garden/Plant Notes:

Date _____

Weather Observations:

Phenological Observations:

Garden/Plant Notes:

Date _____

Weather Observations:

Phenological Observations:

Garden/Plant Notes:

Date _____

Weather Observations:

Phenological Observations:

Garden/Plant Notes:

Date _____

Weather Observations:

Phenological Observations:

Garden/Plant Notes:

Date _____

Weather Observations:

Phenological Observations:

Garden/Plant Notes:

Date _____

Weather Observations:

Phenological Observations:

Garden/Plant Notes:

Date _____

Weather Observations:

Phenological Observations:

Garden/Plant Notes:

Date _____

Weather Observations:

Phenological Observations:

Garden/Plant Notes:

Date _____

Weather Observations:

Phenological Observations:

Garden/Plant Notes:

Date _____

Weather Observations:

Phenological Observations:

Garden/Plant Notes:

Date _____

Weather Observations:

Phenological Observations:

Garden/Plant Notes:

Date _____

Weather Observations:

Phenological Observations:

Garden/Plant Notes:

Date _____

Weather Observations:

Phenological Observations:

Garden/Plant Notes:

Date _____

Weather Observations:

Phenological Observations:

Garden/Plant Notes:

Date _____

Weather Observations:

Phenological Observations:

Garden/Plant Notes:

Date _____

Weather Observations:

Phenological Observations:

Garden/Plant Notes:

Date _____

Weather Observations:

Phenological Observations:

Garden/Plant Notes:

Date _____

Weather Observations:

Phenological Observations:

Garden/Plant Notes:

Date _____

Weather Observations:

Phenological Observations:

Garden/Plant Notes:

Date _____

Weather Observations:

Phenological Observations:

Garden/Plant Notes:

Date _____

Weather Observations:

Phenological Observations:

Garden/Plant Notes:

Date _____

Weather Observations:

Phenological Observations:

Garden/Plant Notes:

Date _____

Weather Observations:

Phenological Observations:

Garden/Plant Notes:

Date _____

Weather Observations:

Phenological Observations:

Garden/Plant Notes:

Date _____

Weather Observations:

Phenological Observations:

Garden/Plant Notes:

Date _____

Weather Observations:

Phenological Observations:

Garden/Plant Notes:

Date _____

Weather Observations:

Phenological Observations:

Garden/Plant Notes:

Date _____

Weather Observations:

Phenological Observations:

Garden/Plant Notes:

Date _____

Weather Observations:

Phenological Observations:

Garden/Plant Notes:

Date _____

Weather Observations:

Phenological Observations:

Garden/Plant Notes:

Date _____

Weather Observations:

Phenological Observations:

Garden/Plant Notes:

Date _____

Weather Observations:

Phenological Observations:

Garden/Plant Notes:

Date _____

Weather Observations:

Phenological Observations:

Garden/Plant Notes:

Date _____

Weather Observations:

Phenological Observations:

Garden/Plant Notes:

Date _____

Weather Observations:

Phenological Observations:

Garden/Plant Notes:

Date _____

Weather Observations:

Phenological Observations:

Garden/Plant Notes:

Date _____

Weather Observations:

Phenological Observations:

Garden/Plant Notes:

Date _____

Weather Observations:

Phenological Observations:

Garden/Plant Notes:

Date _____

Weather Observations:

Phenological Observations:

Garden/Plant Notes:

Date _____

Weather Observations:

Phenological Observations:

Garden/Plant Notes:

Date _____

Weather Observations:

Phenological Observations:

Garden/Plant Notes:

Date _____

Weather Observations:

Phenological Observations:

Garden/Plant Notes:

Date _____

Weather Observations:

Phenological Observations:

Garden/Plant Notes:

Date _____

Weather Observations:

Phenological Observations:

Garden/Plant Notes:

Date _____

Weather Observations:

Phenological Observations:

Garden/Plant Notes:

Date _____

Weather Observations:

Phenological Observations:

Garden/Plant Notes:

Date _____

Weather Observations:

Phenological Observations:

Garden/Plant Notes:

Date _____

Weather Observations:

Phenological Observations:

Garden/Plant Notes:

Date _____

Weather Observations:

Phenological Observations:

Garden/Plant Notes:

Date _____

Weather Observations:

Phenological Observations:

Garden/Plant Notes:

Date _____

Weather Observations:

Phenological Observations:

Garden/Plant Notes:

Date _____

Weather Observations:

Phenological Observations:

Garden/Plant Notes:

Date _____

Weather Observations:

Phenological Observations:

Garden/Plant Notes:

Date _____

Weather Observations:

Phenological Observations:

Garden/Plant Notes:

Date _____

Weather Observations:

Phenological Observations:

Garden/Plant Notes:

Date _____

Weather Observations:

Phenological Observations:

Garden/Plant Notes:

Date _____

Weather Observations:

Phenological Observations:

Garden/Plant Notes:

Date _____

Weather Observations:

Phenological Observations:

Garden/Plant Notes:

Date _____

Weather Observations:

Phenological Observations:

Garden/Plant Notes:

Date _____

Weather Observations:

Phenological Observations:

Garden/Plant Notes:

Date _____

Weather Observations:

Phenological Observations:

Garden/Plant Notes:

Date _____

Weather Observations:

Phenological Observations:

Garden/Plant Notes:

Date _____

Weather Observations:

Phenological Observations:

Garden/Plant Notes:

Date _____

Weather Observations:

Phenological Observations:

Garden/Plant Notes:

Date _____

Weather Observations:

Phenological Observations:

Garden/Plant Notes:

Date _____

Weather Observations:

Phenological Observations:

Garden/Plant Notes:

Date _____

Weather Observations:

Phenological Observations:

Garden/Plant Notes:

Date _____

Weather Observations:

Phenological Observations:

Garden/Plant Notes:

Date _____

Weather Observations:

Phenological Observations:

Garden/Plant Notes:

Date _____

Weather Observations:

Phenological Observations:

Garden/Plant Notes:

Date _____

Weather Observations:

Phenological Observations:

Garden/Plant Notes:

Date _____

Weather Observations:

Phenological Observations:

Garden/Plant Notes:

Date _____

Weather Observations:

Phenological Observations:

Garden/Plant Notes:

Date _____

Weather Observations:

Phenological Observations:

Garden/Plant Notes:

Date _____

Weather Observations:

Phenological Observations:

Garden/Plant Notes:

Date _____

Weather Observations:

Phenological Observations:

Garden/Plant Notes:

Date _____

Weather Observations:

Phenological Observations:

Garden/Plant Notes:

Date _____

Weather Observations:

Phenological Observations:

Garden/Plant Notes:

Date _____

Weather Observations:

Phenological Observations:

Garden/Plant Notes:

Date _____

Weather Observations:

Phenological Observations:

Garden/Plant Notes:

Date _____

Weather Observations:

Phenological Observations:

Garden/Plant Notes:

Date _____

Weather Observations:

Phenological Observations:

Garden/Plant Notes:

Date _____

Weather Observations:

Phenological Observations:

Garden/Plant Notes:

Date _____

Weather Observations:

Phenological Observations:

Garden/Plant Notes:

Date _____

Weather Observations:

Phenological Observations:

Garden/Plant Notes:

Date _____

Weather Observations:

Phenological Observations:

Garden/Plant Notes:

Date _____

Weather Observations:

Phenological Observations:

Garden/Plant Notes:

Date _____

Weather Observations:

Phenological Observations:

Garden/Plant Notes:

Date _____

Weather Observations:

Phenological Observations:

Garden/Plant Notes:

Date _____

Weather Observations:

Phenological Observations:

Garden/Plant Notes:

Date _____

Weather Observations:

Phenological Observations:

Garden/Plant Notes:

Date _____

Weather Observations:

Phenological Observations:

Garden/Plant Notes:

Date _____

Weather Observations:

Phenological Observations:

Garden/Plant Notes:

Date _____

Weather Observations:

Phenological Observations:

Garden/Plant Notes:

Date _____

Weather Observations:

Phenological Observations:

Garden/Plant Notes:

Date _____

Weather Observations:

Phenological Observations:

Garden/Plant Notes:

Date _____

Weather Observations:

Phenological Observations:

Garden/Plant Notes:

Date _____

Weather Observations:

Phenological Observations:

Garden/Plant Notes:

Date _____

Weather Observations:

Phenological Observations:

Garden/Plant Notes:

Date _____

Weather Observations:

Phenological Observations:

Garden/Plant Notes:

Date _____

Weather Observations:

Phenological Observations:

Garden/Plant Notes:

Date _____

Weather Observations:

Phenological Observations:

Garden/Plant Notes:

Date _____

Weather Observations:

Phenological Observations:

Garden/Plant Notes:

Date _____

Weather Observations:

Phenological Observations:

Garden/Plant Notes:

Date _____

Weather Observations:

Phenological Observations:

Garden/Plant Notes:

Date _____

Weather Observations:

Phenological Observations:

Garden/Plant Notes:

Date _____

Weather Observations:

Phenological Observations:

Garden/Plant Notes:

Date _____

Weather Observations:

Phenological Observations:

Garden/Plant Notes:

Date _____

Weather Observations:

Phenological Observations:

Garden/Plant Notes:

Date _____

Weather Observations:

Phenological Observations:

Garden/Plant Notes:

Date _____

Weather Observations:

Phenological Observations:

Garden/Plant Notes:

Date _____

Weather Observations:

Phenological Observations:

Garden/Plant Notes:

Date _____

Weather Observations:

Phenological Observations:

Garden/Plant Notes:

Date _____

Weather Observations:

Phenological Observations:

Garden/Plant Notes:

Date _____

Weather Observations:

Phenological Observations:

Garden/Plant Notes:

Date _____

Weather Observations:

Phenological Observations:

Garden/Plant Notes:

Date _____

Weather Observations:

Phenological Observations:

Garden/Plant Notes:

Date _____

Weather Observations:

Phenological Observations:

Garden/Plant Notes:

Date _____

Weather Observations:

Phenological Observations:

Garden/Plant Notes:

Date _____

Weather Observations:

Phenological Observations:

Garden/Plant Notes:

Date _____

Weather Observations:

Phenological Observations:

Garden/Plant Notes:

Date _____

Weather Observations:

Phenological Observations:

Garden/Plant Notes:

Date _____

Weather Observations:

Phenological Observations:

Garden/Plant Notes:

Date _____

Weather Observations:

Phenological Observations:

Garden/Plant Notes:

Date _____

Weather Observations:

Phenological Observations:

Garden/Plant Notes:

Date _____

Weather Observations:

Phenological Observations:

Garden/Plant Notes:

Date _____

Weather Observations:

Phenological Observations:

Garden/Plant Notes:

Date _____

Weather Observations:

Phenological Observations:

Garden/Plant Notes:

Date _____

Weather Observations:

Phenological Observations:

Garden/Plant Notes:

Date _____

Weather Observations:

Phenological Observations:

Garden/Plant Notes:

Date _____

Weather Observations:

Phenological Observations:

Garden/Plant Notes:

Date _____

Weather Observations:

Phenological Observations:

Garden/Plant Notes:

Date _____

Weather Observations:

Phenological Observations:

Garden/Plant Notes:

Date _____

Weather Observations:

Phenological Observations:

Garden/Plant Notes:

Date _____

Weather Observations:

Phenological Observations:

Garden/Plant Notes:

Date _____

Weather Observations:

Phenological Observations:

Garden/Plant Notes:

Date _____

Weather Observations:

Phenological Observations:

Garden/Plant Notes:

Date _____

Weather Observations:

Phenological Observations:

Garden/Plant Notes:

Date _____

Weather Observations:

Phenological Observations:

Garden/Plant Notes:

Date _____

Weather Observations:

Phenological Observations:

Garden/Plant Notes:

Date _____

Weather Observations:

Phenological Observations:

Garden/Plant Notes:

Date _____

Weather Observations:

Phenological Observations:

Garden/Plant Notes:

Date _____

Weather Observations:

Phenological Observations:

Garden/Plant Notes:

Date _____

Weather Observations:

Phenological Observations:

Garden/Plant Notes:

Date _____

Weather Observations:

Phenological Observations:

Garden/Plant Notes:

Date _____

Weather Observations:

Phenological Observations:

Garden/Plant Notes:

Date _____

Weather Observations:

Phenological Observations:

Garden/Plant Notes:

Date _____

Weather Observations:

Phenological Observations:

Garden/Plant Notes:

Date _____

Weather Observations:

Phenological Observations:

Garden/Plant Notes:

Date _____

Weather Observations:

Phenological Observations:

Garden/Plant Notes:

Date _____

Weather Observations:

Phenological Observations:

Garden/Plant Notes:

Date _____

Weather Observations:

Phenological Observations:

Garden/Plant Notes:

Date _____

Weather Observations:

Phenological Observations:

Garden/Plant Notes:

Date _____

Weather Observations:

Phenological Observations:

Garden/Plant Notes:

Date _____

Weather Observations:

Phenological Observations:

Garden/Plant Notes:

Date _____

Weather Observations:

Phenological Observations:

Garden/Plant Notes:

Date _____

Weather Observations:

Phenological Observations:

Garden/Plant Notes:

Date _____

Weather Observations:

Phenological Observations:

Garden/Plant Notes:

Date _____

Weather Observations:

Phenological Observations:

Garden/Plant Notes:

Date _____

Weather Observations:

Phenological Observations:

Garden/Plant Notes:

Date _____

Weather Observations:

Phenological Observations:

Garden/Plant Notes:

Date _____

Weather Observations:

Phenological Observations:

Garden/Plant Notes:

Date _____

Weather Observations:

Phenological Observations:

Garden/Plant Notes:

Date _____

Weather Observations:

Phenological Observations:

Garden/Plant Notes:

Pest and Disease Problems

Many home gardeners began growing their own fruits and vegetables just to get away from the chemical-tainted food produced by U.S. agribusiness. Biological or natural methods of pest control and disease prevention call for recorded observations on the gardener's part to work most effectively. Phenological observations help many farmers and gardeners know when certain insect attacks will come. In Montana, farmers who make the first cut of alfalfa within ten days of the beginning of bloom of the common purple lilac remove the alfalfa weevil eggs. North Carolinians can avoid widespread damage by cabbage maggots to brassica plants by delaying planting time until the dogwood is in full bloom. On Long Island the cabbage maggot adults arrive about the time the forsythia is in full bloom, and county agricultural agents advise gardeners to watch the forsythia and key their planting to its bloom.

Phenological observations (see the previous section) can help you pinpoint times of insect infestations and other plant damage. For example, deer damage to young apple trees is often linked to the time when young fawns just begin to move out through the meadows at night. Their browsing ravages seem to coincide with the period when the tender new growth on young fruit trees is most succulent and lush. Hair bags, fencing, and a dog in the orchard can be very helpful, especially if you know when to expect the raids.

Companion planting, insecticidal soaps, insect predators, botanical sprays, mechanical collection of harmful insects, bacterial sprays, pheromone traps, and sticky stakes and tags are all weapons in the organic gardener's arsenal, but the effectiveness of most of these depends on the gardener's personal knowledge of insect habits, cycles, peak populations, and growth stages and knowing what attracts them. Chemicals appeal to farmers and gardeners because they are easy—no observation, no records, no thinking—just dump the stuff on. Biological controls demand more from the gardener.

Learn to identify what is eating your crops—insects, deer, woodchucks, red squirrels, or chickens—record the date, the weather, stage of plant growth, type of garden plan (large blocks of one type of plant are very attractive to predators, while interplantings or small scattered groups are often ignored); note the extent of the damage and the steps you take to prevent it happening again, and, finally, the results. Good records can help you be prepared for the attack next year and even to ward it off.

Know the Enemy

Anna Carr's *Rodale's Color Handbook of Garden Insects* (Emmaus, Pa.: Rodale Press, 1979) is one of the best insect identification books for gardeners and has a good bibliography if you get interested in entomology beyond the call of plant protection. Listed after each insect are tested natural controls. You may want to add sketches or your own photographs of marauding insects in your garden not discoverable in the book. Brooklyn Botanic Garden Handbooks No. 34, *Biological Control of Plant Pests,* and No. 89, *Gardening without Pests,* both contain good material on several methods of controlling plant-feeding garden insects.

Plant breeders in the past decades have concentrated increasingly on developing vegetable and fruit cultivars resistant to disease and insect damage. The careful seed and plant shopper can save much trouble by choosing such seed and stock to plant. Watch for disease-resistant varieties as you study the seed catalogs. An important source of disease-resistant apple trees (apples demand more spray applications, up to 15 in one season, than any other crop) is:

The New York State Fruit Testing Cooperative Association, Inc., Box 462, Geneva, NY 14456.

Companion Planting

The effectiveness of companion plantings is still a lively issue, and much research still needs to be done on the subject. Home gardeners can do their own observational research. There are half a dozen books listing hundreds of plant combinations that enhance each other's growth or repel voracious insects. Yet an article in the Brooklyn Botanic Garden Handbook No. 77, *Natural Gardening Handbook,* entitled "Companionate Plantings— Do They Work?" by S. G. Gesell et al., reported on a Pennsylvania study of the effectiveness of six plants in preventing damage by particular insects when planted as companions to six certain vegetables. The study showed no measurable protection from insect damage. Quite different views are found in Helen Philbrick and Richard B. Gregg's *Companion Plants and How to Use Them* (Old Greenwich, Conn.: Devin-Adair Co., 1966), which includes recipes for insect-repelling herb teas.

A good summary of crop rotation as companion planting *over time* is found in John Jeavons' *How to Grow More Vegetables.* Audrey Wynne Hatfield's *How to Enjoy Your Weeds* (New York: Sterling Publishing Co., 1971) is also useful to gardeners interested in companion planting.

Diversified intercropping is widely recognized as very beneficial in the garden, and crop rotation discourages overwintering insects; both of these techniques can be described as forms of companion planting. The reasons why certain plants seem to do well in the company of others can be quite complex and involve many interrelated factors, from root exudates to environmental features. Careful records of companion plantings in your garden measured against control plants grown without the companion can do much to tell you what really works with *your* cultivars in *your* garden and *your* climate.

A comprehensive reference book useful to organic gardeners is *Organic Plant Protection,* edited by Roger B. Yepsen, Jr. (Emmaus, Pa.: Rodale Press, 1976).

Organic Controls

"Soap" mixtures of fatty acids are increasingly recognized as toxic to such plant pests as spider mites, aphids, whiteflies, and mealybugs without harming bees or ladybugs. These mixtures are biodegradable and harmless to plants. The first on the market is Safer Agro-Chem Insecticidal Soap, made by:

Safer Agro-Chem, 13910 Lyons Valley Rd., Jamul, CA 92035. This mixture can be ordered from garden and horticultural suppliers.

There are a number of natural insecticides. One, ryania, is a very potent insecticide made from the roots of a tropical shrub. This and other botanical sprays such as rotenone and pyrethrum are available from mail-order suppliers and garden centers. Pheromone traps, sticky stakes and hanging sticky bars, *Bacillus thuringiensis,* milky spore bacteria, and other natural pest controls can be ordered from Mellinger's, which has a good inventory of organic controls:

Mellinger's, 2310 W. South Range Rd., North Lima, OH 44452.

A new whitefly biological control, the parasitic wasp *Encarsia formosa,* can be ordered from:

Whitefly Control Co., Box 986, Milpitas, CA 95035. Send a self-addressed stamped envelope for further information.

There is also Japanese beetle news on the horizon. The Ohio Agricultural Research and Development Center in Wooster, Ohio, after a decade of study, has linked Japanese beetle populations to acid soil pH readings. Liming at the rate of 100 pounds per 1,000 square feet apparently discourages the beetles from depositing their eggs in the soil.

Pest and Disease Record

Pest or Disease	Date First Observed	Plant Host	Stage of Development		Garden Notes
			Plant	Insect	

Details of Damage	Preventives	Results

The Gardener's Library

One of the most pleasant and worthwhile hobbies the gardener can cultivate is collecting and reading books that suit his or her horticultural interests, whether they lie in scented geraniums, water lilies, herbs, pumpkins, or early threshing machines. Many of the nineteenth-century books on subjects from asparagus to zebra plants are rich in information that is not only historically interesting, but often still useful. If you are attracted to book collecting, rural agrarian works are still temptingly modest in price.

For a list of dealers specializing in antiquarian horticultural works, write:

The Antiquarian Booksellers' Association, 630 Fifth Ave., New York, NY 10020.

Here are some of the booksellers who deal in old garden catalogs, pamphlets, horticultural prints, and a great range of books of interest to the gardener:

G. A. Bibby, 714 Pleasant St., Roseville, CA 95678. Gardening and horticultural books.

Horticultural Books Inc., 219 Martin Ave., Stuart, FL 33494. Gardening books.

Second Life Books, Upper East Hoosac St., Adams, MA 01220. Books on agriculture and horticulture.

The Printer's Devil, 1 Claremont Ct., Arlington, MA 02174. Gardening books.

Edward C. Fales, Turnpike Rd., Salisbury, NH 03268.

Gardening books.

HHH Horticultural, 68 Brooktree Rd., Hightstown, NJ 08520. HHH specializes in new gardening and horticultural books.

Elizabeth Woodburn, Booknoll Farm, Hopewell, NJ 08525. An outstanding collection of old and rare material is offered by this distinguished dealer who specializes in American agricultural history.

Pomona Book Exchange, 33 Beaucourt Rd., Toronto, ON L0R 1X0, Canada. Pomona deals in books on edible plants—grains, fungi, vegetables, fruits, nuts, and others.

The Massachusetts Horticultural Society offers hundreds of horticultural books for sale through the shop or mail. Write:

MHS, Gardener's Library, 300 Massachusetts Ave., Boston, MA 02115.

The pages that follow can be used to catalog your book collection, start a "wish list" of books you want to buy, keep track of books loaned to friends, or jot down names and addresses of sources for old books in your area.

Gardeners' Cookbooks

One type of book collection of particular interest to all vegetable and fruit growers is a kitchen library devoted to the edible fruits of your gardening labors. In a year of bountiful harvest, even a master chef can go somewhat gaga trying to keep ahead of the zucchini and string beans. Fortunately, part of the surge of interest in gardening in the last decade has given us some marvelous cookery books specializing in vegetables and fruits. Local food co-ops, libraries, and bookstores are good places to check for cookbooks that suit your style and garden. Here are some of the best of the crop:

Robert Ackart, *Fruits in Cooking: Unusual and Classic Fruit Recipes.* New York: Macmillan, 1973. This is an outstanding cookbook that belongs on the shelves of everyone who grows orchard or small fruits.

Edward Espé Brown, *Tassajara Cooking.* Boulder, Colo.: Shambala Publications, Inc. (dist. by Random House), 1973. Kitchen techniques, reverence for the earth, respect for vegetables, and aesthetically pleasing vegetable recipes make this vegetarian cookbook quite unusual.

Derek Fell and Phyllis Shaudys, *The Complete Vegetable Spaghetti Cookbook.* Washington's Crossing, Pa.: Pine Row Publications. (Order from the authors at $4.95.)

Marion Gorman, *Cooking with Fruit.* Emmaus, Pa.: Rodale Press, 1983. A collection of elegant recipes for a broad range of fruits, both common and exotic.

Nika Hazelton, *The Unabridged Vegetable Cookbook.* New York: M. Evans & Co., 1976. Although this book was written for supermarket shoppers, its unusual and excellent recipes are of great use for gardeners.

Ruth Herzberg et al., *The New Putting Food By.* Brattleboro, Vt.: Stephen Greene Press, 1982. The updated version of the earlier encyclopedia of food preservation.

Mollie Katzen, *The Moosewood Cookbook.* Berkeley, Calif.: Ten Speed Press, 1977. Named for the famous natural foods restaurant, this book presents extraor-dinarily delicious recipes, including many for vegetable dishes.

Milo Miloradovich, *The Art of Cooking with Herbs and Spices.* Garden City, N.Y.: Doubleday & Co., 1952. An older book long out of print, but still one of the best books on the culinary uses of herbs, despite the recent flood of herb cookery books.

Editors of *Organic Gardening and Farming, The Green Thumb Cookbook.* Emmaus, Pa.: Rodale Press, 1977. An assortment of recipes for 61 different vegetables, along with notes on harvesting.

Laurel Robertson et al., *Laurel's Kitchen.* Berkeley, Calif.: Nilgiri Press, 1976. Down-home cooking of the best and most nutritional kind, contains lots of recipes for vegetable dishes that are natural and simple.

James Houston Turner, *The Spud Book: 101 Ways to Cook Potatoes.* New York: St. Martin's Press, 1982. At last, the wonderful potato has a book of its own.

Betty Wason, *The Art of Vegetarian Cookery.* New York: Ace Publishing Co., 1965. Out of print but worth looking for; the chapters on vegetable main dishes contain some of the best recipes anywhere. The sophisticated herb sauces are outstanding.

You can use pages 194 and 195 to catalog the cookbooks you own already, and perhaps even note your favorite vegetable and fruit recipes from each one. These pages can also accommodate a "wish list" of books you want to purchase or read.

Old Cookbooks

Older cookbooks out of print can be found at second-hand bookstores and flea markets, and through booksellers. Barbara L. Feret, Worthington Rd., Huntington, MA 01050, specializes in old cookery books.

Books

Cookbooks

House Plants

Indoor gardening is a complex subject with a set of problems and goals completely different from those of outdoor gardening. The scope of the indoor gardener can be vast, from a concentration on terrariums to orchids to greenhouse vegetable growing to interior landscaping. The following pages provide space to list your house plants. A basic and indispensable aid to lovers of house plants is *Rodale's Encyclopedia of Indoor Gardening,* edited by Anne M. Halpin (Emmaus, Pa.: Rodale Press, 1980). The Brooklyn Botanic Garden has several excellent handbooks for house gardeners: No. 40, *House Plants;* No. 42, *Greenhouse Handbook for the Amateur;* No. 43, *Succulents;* No. 53, *African Violets and Their Relatives;* No. 54, *Orchids;* No. 62, *Gardening Under Artificial Light;* No. 70, *The House Plant Primer;* and No. 75, *Breeding Plants for Home and Garden.*

A very useful small pamphlet is *Success with House Plants Starts with Soil,* published by the Ringer Corporation, Eden Prairie, MN 55344. This pamphlet give five basic potting soil recipes for different groups of house plants.

Many of the plant societies listed on page 70 publish books and pamphlets on the culture of their special groups of plants. The American Orchid Society, for example, puts out several excellent guides, as does the Indoor Light Gardening Society of America. These publications can generally be ordered by mail, by nonmembers as well as members. Here are more helpful books:

Charles Marden Fitch, *The Complete Book of Miniature Roses.* New York: Hawthorn Books, 1977.

Mulford B. Foster, *Bromeliads: A Cultural Handbook.* Orlando, Fla.: The Bromeliad Society, Inc., 1953.

Charles Glass and Robert Foster, *Cacti and Succulents for the Amateur.* New York: Van Nostrand Reinhold Co., 1976.

Barbara J. Hoshizaki, *Fern Growers Manual.* New York: Alfred A. Knopf, 1975.

Elvin McDonald, *The Complete Book of Gardening under Lights.* New York: Popular Library, 1974.

Rebecca Tyson Northern, *Home Orchid Growing.* New York: Van Nostrand Reinhold Co., 1970.

Victoria Padilla, *The Bromeliads.* New York: Crown Publishers, 1973.

Mildred and Edward Thompson, *Begonias: The Complete Reference Guide.* New York: Times Books, 1982.

Use the next two pages to list your indoor plants and make notes on their growth and behavior. Be sure to note the cultivar name and where you obtained the plant. These notes will be a great help to you in remembering your plants' periodic maintenance needs. Instead of attempting to commit to memory the date a plant was last repotted, for instance, you can simply refer to your records to find out.

House Plant Record

Plant	Habit	Source	Propagation	Cultural Notes

Plant	Habit	Source	Propagation	Cultural Notes

Flower Shows and Gardens

Traveling gardeners usually end up wandering through botanical parks and peering at the luscious blooms of local garden shows or enjoying tea and crumpets at house and garden tours in strange towns and cities. More and more travel agencies and tour offices are arranging horticultural tours in this country and abroad—tours of orchid jungles, of the redwood forests, of Dutch bulb shows, of English gardens. Horticultural and gardening periodicals list tours and horticultural exhibitions. If you go, it is useful to bring a small notebook to record your impressions and note the names of outstanding plants. Later on, you can transfer the notes to the pages that follow here, and you'll have a permanent record to look back at in years to come.

There are numerous public botanic gardens and conservatories throughout the United States that are a delight to visit, especially on a cold winter day. Here is a list of some of them:

Desert Botanical Garden, Galvin Pkwy., Papago Park, Phoenix, AZ 85010.

Arizona-Sonora Desert Museum, Rt. 9, Box 900, Tucson, AZ 85702.

Los Angeles State and County Arboretum, 301 N. Baldwin Ave., Arcadia, CA 91006.

University of California Botanic Garden, Centennial Dr., Berkeley, CA 94720.

The Conservatory of Flowers, Golden Gate Park, San Francisco, CA 94117.

Huntington Botanical Gardens, 1151 Oxford Rd., San Marino, CA 91108.

Denver Botanic Gardens, 909 York St., Denver, CO 80206.

United States Botanic Garden, Maryland Ave. and 1st St. SW, Washington, DC 20024.

United States National Arboretum, 24th St. and R St. NE, Washington, DC 20002.

Fairchild Tropical Gardens, 10901 Old Cutler Rd., Miami, FL 33156.

Marie Selby Botanical Gardens, 800 S. Palm Ave., Sarasota, FL 33577.

Garfield Park Conservatory, 300 N. Central Blvd., Chicago, IL 60624.

Chicago Horticultural Society Botanical Garden, Lake Cook Rd., P.O. Box 400, Glencoe, IL 60022.

The Arnold Arboretum of Harvard University, The Arbor Way, Jamaica Plain, MA 02130.

Matthaei Botanical Gardens, University of Michigan, 1800 N. Dixboro Rd., Ann Arbor, MI 48105.

Missouri Botanical Garden, 2101 Tower Grove Ave., St. Louis, MO 63110.

New York Botanical Garden, Bronx Park, Bronx, NY 10458.

Brooklyn Botanic Garden, 1000 Washington Ave., Brooklyn, NY 11225.

North Carolina Botanical Gardens, University of North Carolina, Chapel Hill, NC 27514.

The Garden Center of Greater Cleveland, 11030 East Blvd., Cleveland, OH 44106.

Hoyt Arboretum, 4000 S.W. Fairview Blvd., Portland, OR 97221.

Longwood Gardens, Kennett Square, PA 19348.

Phipps Conservatory, Schenley Park, Pittsburgh, PA 15213.

The Tennessee Botanical Gardens and Fine Arts Center, Cheekwood, Nashville, TN 37205.

River Farm, American Horticultural Society, 7931 E. Boulevard Dr., Alexandria, VA 22308.

Norfolk Botanical Gardens, Airport Rd., Norfolk, VA 23518.

Montreal Botanic Garden, 4101 est. rue Sherbrooke, Montreal, PQ H1X 2B2, Canada.

An indispensable traveler's guide is the Brooklyn Botanic Garden Handbook No. 64, *American Gardens— A Traveler's Guide,* with detailed listings of 250 gardens and arboretums in the United States and Canada. Useful to visitors to New England is R. R. Payne's *New England Gardens Open to the Public* (Boston: David R. Godine, 1979).

There are major flower shows each year in Boston, Baltimore, Philadelphia, Chicago, and a number of other cities. In addition, many local and regional horticultural and plant societies sponsor lovely shows. Growing plants to show is a challenging and rewarding activity, and throughout the year some of these groups also hold classes and seminars on how to select and prepare the best specimens from your indoor garden for entry in a show.

An extraordinary display of forced bulbs in an ornate container.

Flower Shows

Gardens Visited

The Gardener's Tool Chest

The best-quality garden tools are a pleasure to work with, last several lifetimes, and get the work well done. A tool made of good steel holds an edge longer than a cheap junk tool. Spades and shovels should have metal shanks extending up the handles for greater strength. One-piece stamped metal trowels gradually flex, bend, and break, where those with a sturdy wooden handle last a long time and give good service. Garden tools—shovels, hoes, trowels—should be kept sharp. Sharpen both edges with a large bastard file. Wooden handles should have a broad band of bright-colored paint to make them visible when they are lying on the ground, and for easy identification if you are the kindly gardener who lends tools out.

Tools should be cleaned off before they are put away in the tool house. A wooden tool scraper cleans fresh soil away in a few vigorous minutes. Garden hoses should be drained, reeled, and put away when not in use. Letting hoses lie for long periods in the sun makes them deteriorate rapidly. Soaker hose and irrigation lines need to be cleaned and put away carefully in the fall. Spray cans should be rinsed after every use and stored upside down. Both tillers and lawn mowers should be cleaned at the end of the season before they are stored. Exposed metal on these machines should be coated lightly with a film of oil. Run these machines until all the gasoline in the tank, line, and carburetor is exhausted, for gasoline that stands for months leaves a thick, clogging residue as it evaporates. Read storage directions for your tiller; you may need to drain the oil and remove the spark plugs. Clean all empty plant pots thoroughly, and let them dry a day in the sun before storing them in the potting shed upside down.

Several outstanding sources of superior garden tools are:

Smith & Hawken Tool Company, 68 Homer, Palo Alto, CA 94301.

Gardener's Eden, 25 Huntington at Copley, Boston, MA 02116.

Brookstone Company, 70 Vose Farm Rd., Peterborough, NH 03458.

Hand & Foot, Ltd., Box 611, Brattleboro, VT 05301. Source of an outstanding garden cart.

A list of tools and their purchase dates can be a helpful record in case of loss. Use the next page for your tool inventory, and also to note any tools you lend out to friends and neighbors.

Tool List

Tool	Source	Date Purchased